GERMA

M. McAleavy

Head of Modern Languages,
Sydney Smith School, Hull

CASSELL

Cassell Publishers Ltd
Artillery House
Artillery Row
London
SW1P 1RT

First published 1989

ISBN 0-304-31623-7

British Library Cataloguing in Publication Data
McAleavy, M.
Cassell's German wordlist.
1. German language. German & English dictionaries
I. Title
433′.21

Typeset in Century Schoolbook by Witwell Ltd, Southport

Printed in Great Britain by Anchor Press Ltd, Tiptree, Essex

To the Teacher, Pupil and Parent

All the GCSE board have issued vocabulary lists on which they will base their exams. No questions may be asked which require knowledge of words not on the lists.

Unfortunately, no English translation is provided with these lists and this leaves teachers in a quandary as to how to exploit them. I, like many of my colleagues, have faced continual demands from pupils for a translation and these have led me to write this book.

This GCSE vocabulary book is based on the vocabulary lists provided by the GCSE exam boards. It has been structured to cover the vocabulary lists of each and every board and the requirements of Standard Grade. Very simple words, unlikely words and some words which are the same in English have been omitted.

We are now being forced to use a number of different books to cover the four skill areas of listening, speaking, reading and writing. Few (if any) have a comprehensive German/ English and English/German vocabulary list. Few (if any) of the major course-books have such a list. I am sure that GCSE and Standard Grade students of all ages will find this book a valuable companion as it provides both.

Space has been provided for any additional words that you might like to insert. Words like 'match' have been contextualised so that you know whether you are referring to a football match or a match for lighting a fire.

For reasons of space, in general only the masculine forms for inhabitants of countries, professions and occupations have been given. Pupils may need to be reminded to add '-in' to the noun to form the feminine equivalent, eg

MASC.	*FEM.*
der Lehrer	die Lehrerin

An asterisk denotes a separable verb.

Numbers — die Zahlen (*f pl*)

Cardinal numbers — *die Kardinalzahlen*

0 null	11 elf	21 einundzwanzig
1 eins	12 zwölf	22 zweiundzwanzig
2 zwei	13 dreizehn	30 dreißig
3 drei	14 vierzehn	40 vierzig
4 vier	15 fünfzehn	50 fünfzig
5 fünf	16 sechzehn	60 sechzig
6 sechs	17 siebzehn	70 siebzig
7 sieben	18 achtzehn	80 achtzig
8 acht	19 neunzehn	89 neunzig
9 neun	20 zwanzig	100 hundert
10 zehn		

101	hunderteins	5,000	fünftausend
102	hundertzwei	1,001	tausendeins
200	zweihundert	1,000,000	eine Million
1000	tausend		

Ordinal numbers — *die Ordinalzahlen*

first	erste	eleventh	elfte
second	zweite	twelfth	zwölfte
third	dritte	thirteenth	dreizehnte
fourth	vierte	fourteenth	vierzehnte
fifth	fünfte	fifteenth	fünfzehnte
sixth	sechste	sixteenth	sechzehnte
seventh	sieb(en)te	seventeenth	siebzehnte
eight	achte	eighteenth	achtzehnte
ninth	neunte	nineteenth	neunzehnte
tenth	zehnte	twentieth	zwanzigste
		twenty-first	einund-zwanzigste
		fiftieth	fünfzigste
		hundredth	hundertste

The days of the week — Die Tage (*m pl*) der Woche

Monday	Montag
Tuesday	Dienstag
Wednesday	Mittwoch
Thursday	Donnerstag

Friday	Freitag
Saturday	Samstag/Sonnabend
Sunday	Sonntag
today	heute
yesterday	gestern
tomorrow	morgen
the day before yesterday	vorgestern
the day after tomorrow	übermorgen
the day before	am vorigen/ vorhergehenden Tag
the next day	am nächsten/ folgenden Tag
on Friday	am Freitag
on Tuesday	dienstags
every Wednesday	jeden Mittwoch
in the morning	morgens
in the afternoon	nachmittags
in the evening	abends
at night	nachts

The months — **Die Monate** (*m pl*)

January	Januar	July	Juli
February	Februar	August	August
March	März	September	September
April	April	October	Oktober
May	Mai	November	November
June	Juni	December	Dezember

in September	im September
What's the date today?	Den wievielten haben wir heute? Der wievielte ist heute?
Today is/it's the first day of May	Wir haben den ersten Mai Heute/Es ist der erste Mai
It's the twentieth	Es ist der zwanzigste
It's the seventh of June (1992)	Es ist der siebente Juni (neunzehnhundertzweiundneunzig)

The seasons — **Die Jahreszeiten** (*f pl*)

Spring	der Frühling

Summer	der Sommer
Autumn	der Herbst
Winter	der Winter
in spring/summer/ autumn/winter	im Frühling/Sommer/ Herbst /Winter

The time	**Die Zeit**
What's the time?	Wieviel Uhr ist es?
What time is it?	Wie spät ist es/haben Sie's?
It's seven o'clock	Es ist sieben Uhr
It's five minutes past two	Es ist fünf (Minuten) nach zwei/zwei Uhr fünf
It's a quarter past/ to nine	Es ist Viertel nach/ vor neun
It's half past four	Es ist halb fünf/vier Uhr dreißig
It's twenty to six	Es ist zwanzig vor sechs/ fünf Uhr vierzig
It's twelve o'clock/noon/ midnight	Es ist Mittag/zwölf Uhrt (mittags)/Mitternacht/ zwölf Uhr nachts
At 16.25	Um sechzehn Uhr fünfundzwanzig
At 14.45	Um vierzehn Uhr fünfundvierzig
At 18.00	Um achtzehn Uhr
a.m.	morgens/vormittags
p.m.	nachmittags
p.m. (after five 5 p.m.)	abends
at five o'clock in the morning	um fünf Uhr morgens

The weather	**Das Wetter**
What's the weather like?	Wie ist das Wetter?
It's hot/cold/cool	Es ist heiß/kalt/kühl
It's sunny/windy	Es ist sonnig/windig
It's raining/snowing	Es regnet/schneit
It's freezing/thawing	Es friert/taut
It's foggy	Es ist neb(e)lig
The weather is fine/bad	Das Wetter ist schön/ schlecht

Prepositions

With Accusative		*With Dative*	
bis	until	aus	from, out of
durch	through	außer	apart from
entlang	along	bei	with, at the house of
für	for		
gegen	against	gegenüber	opposite
ohne	without	mit	with
um	around, at (time)	nach	to, after
		seit	since, for
		von	from, by
		zu	to

With Accusative and Dative

an	at, to	über	over, across, above, via
auf	on, onto		
hinter	behind	unter	under
in	in, into	vor	before, in front of
neben	next to	zwischen	between

With Genitive

statt	instead of	während	during
trotz	in spite of	wegen	because of

Conjunctions

Co-ordinating Conjunctions

aber	but	sondern	but
denn	for	und	and
oder	or		

Subordinating Conjunctions

als	when	obwohl	although
bevor	before	seitdem	since
bis	until	während	whilst
da	since	weil	because
damit	so that	wenn	when, if
daß	that	wo	where
nachdem	after		

Where a word has several possible usages, only the meaning or meanings most appropriate to GCSE have been given.

There is a section at the front covering numbers, days, months, seasons, time, weather, prepositions and conjunctions.

Viel Spaß!

M. McAleavy
Head of Modern Languages, Sydney Smith School, Hull

I would like to thank my wife Lesley, for her patience, understanding and help, and also Steve for introducing me to the intricate world of the word-processor.

abbiegen*	to turn off (the road, etc)
der **Abend** (e)	evening
das **Abendbrot** (e)	supper
das **Abendessen** (-)	evening meal
das **Abenteuer** (-)	adventure
abfahren*	to depart
die **Abfahrt** (en)	departure
der **Abfall** (¨e)	litter
abhängen* von	to depend on
abholen*	to fetch; to meet
das **Abitur**	A-levels
ablehnen*	to refuse
abnehmen*	to take off, to lose weight
abräumen*	to clear away
abschleppen*	to tow away
abschließen*	to lock up
die **Abschlußprüfung** (en)	final examination
abschreiben*	to copy
der **Absender** (-)	sender
Abstand halten	to keep one's distance
das **Abteil** (e)	compartment
die **Abteilung** (en)	department
abwaschen*	to wash up
abwesend	absent
achten auf	to pay attention to
Achtung!	Attention!
der **ADAC**	German Automobile Club
die **Adresse** (n)	address

der **Affe** (n)	monkey
ähnlich	similar
die **Ahnung** (en)	idea
aktuell	current
der **Alkohol**	alcohol
allein	alone
alles	everything
alles Gute	all the best
allgemein	common; general
als	than
also	so, thus
alt	old
das **Alter** (-)	age
Amerika/Amerikaner	America/American
amerikanisch	American
die **Ampel** (n)	traffic lights
die **Ananas** (-se)	pineapple
der **Apparat** (e)	apparatus
an Bord	on board
anbieten*	to offer
das **Andenken** (-)	souvenir
ander-	other
anders	different
anderthalb	one and a half
der **Anfang** (¨-e)	start
anfangen*	to start
angeben*	to give (details, etc)
angeln	to fish
die **Angelrute** (n)	fishing-rod
angenehm	pleasant
der/die **Angestellte** (n)	employee
die **Angst** (¨-e)	fear

anhaben*	to have on (clothes)
ankommen*	to arrive
die **Ankunft** (¨e)	arrival
anlassen*	to start (engine)
Anlieger frei	Access only
anmachen*	to turn on
die **Anmeldung** (en)	reception (Youth Hostel, etc)
annehmen*	to accept
der **Anorak** (s)	anorak
anprobieren*	to try on
der **Anruf** (e)	telephone call
anrufen*	to call up
der **Ansager** (-)	announcer
die **Anschrift** (en)	address
ansehen*	to look at
die **Ansichtskarte** (n)	picture postcard
die **Anstrengung** (en)	exertion
die **Antwort** (en)	answer
antworten	to answer
anziehen*	to put on (clothes)
sich **anziehen***	to get dressed
der **Anzug** (¨e)	suit
der **Apfel** (¨)	apple
der **Apfelsaft**	apple juice
die **Apfelsine** (n)	orange
die **Apotheke** (n)	chemist's shop
die **Arbeit** (en)	work
arbeiten	to work
der **Arbeiter** (-)	worker
der **Arbeitgeber** (-)	employer
der **Arbeitnehmer** (-)	employee

arbeitslos	unemployed
sich **ärgern**	to get annoyed
arm	poor
der **Arm** (e)	arm
die **Armbanduhr** (en)	wristwatch
die **Art** (en)	type
der **Artikel** (-)	article
der **Arzt** (¨-e)	doctor
der **Aschenbecher** (-)	ashtray
atemlos	breathless
auch	also
auf Wiederhören	goodbye (on telephone)
auf Wiedersehen	goodbye
der **Aufenthalt** (e)	stay
die **Aufführung** (en)	performance
die **Aufgabe** (n)	task
aufgeben*	to give up
aufhören*	to stop
aufmachen*	to open
die **Aufnahme** (n)	photograph
aufpassen* (auf)	to take care (of)
aufräumen*	to tidy up
der **Aufsatz** (¨-e)	essay
der **Aufschnitt**	slices of cold meat
aufstehen*	to get up
aufwachen*	to wake up
der **Aufzug** (¨-e)	lift
das **Auge** (n)	eye
der **Augenblick** (e)	moment
die **Aula** (Aulen)	school hall
der **Ausdruck** (¨-e)	expression

die **Ausfahrt** (en)	exit (road)
der **Ausflug** (¨e)	excursion
der **Ausgang** (¨e)	exit (building)
ausgeben*	to spend (money)
ausgehen*	to go out
ausgezeichnet	excellent
die **Auskunft** (¨e)	information
das **Ausland**	abroad
der **Ausländer** (-)	foreigner
ausmachen*	to turn off (the light, etc)
auspacken*	to unpack
ausreichend	sufficient
sich **ausruhen***	to have a rest
ausschalten*	to turn off (the light, etc)
aussehen*	to look (i.e. appear)
außer Betrieb	out of order
die **Aussicht** (en)	view
aussprechen*	to pronounce
aussteigen*	to get off/out
die **Ausstellung** (en)	exhibition
der **Ausstieg** (e)	exit (bus, etc)
der **Austausch** (e)	exchange
der **Ausverkauf**	sale
ausverkauft	sold out
die **Auswahl** (en)	selection
ausziehen*	to take off
sich **ausziehen***	to get undressed
das **Auto** (s)	car
die **Autobahn** (en)	motorway
der **Automat** (en)	machine (vending)

das **Baby** (s)	baby
der **Bach** (¨e)	stream
backen	to bake
der **Bäcker** (-)	baker
die **Bäckerei** (en)	bakery
das **Bad** (¨er)	bath
der **Badeanzug** (¨e)	bathing costume
die **Badehose** (n)	swimming trunks
die **Bademütze** (n)	swimming cap
baden	to bathe
das **Badetuch** (¨er)	bath towel
die **Badewanne** (n)	bath-tub
das **Badezimmer** (-)	bathroom
der **Bahnhof** (¨e)	station
der **Bahnsteig** (e)	platform
der **Bahnübergang** (¨e)	railway crossing
bald	soon
der **Balkon** (e)	balcony
der **Ball** (¨e)	ball
die **Banane** (n)	banana
die **Bank** (¨e)	bench
die **Bank** (en)	bank
der **Bart** (¨e)	beard
basteln	to tinker; do handicrafts
die **Batterie** (n)	battery
der **Bauch** (¨e)	belly
bauen	to build
der **Bauer** (n)	farmer
der **Bauernhof** (¨e)	farm
der **Baum** (¨e)	tree
die **Baumwolle**	cotton

die **Baustelle** (n)	building site
der **Beamte** (n)	official
beantworten	to answer
bedeckt	overcast; covered
bedeuten	to mean
sich **bedienen**	to help oneself
die **Bedienung**	service
sich **beeilen**	to hurry
beenden	to end
befehlen	to order (give commands)
sich **befinden**	to be situated
befriedigend	satisfactory
beginnen	to begin
begleiten	to accompany
begrüßen	to greet
behandeln	to treat
beide	both
beilegen*	to enclose
das **Bein** (e)	leg
das **Beispiel** (e)	example
beißen	to bite
der/die **Bekannte** (n)	acquaintance
sich **beklagen**	to complain
bekommen	to get
belegtes Brot	sandwich
Belgien/Belgier	Belgium/Belgian
belgisch	Belgian
beliebt	popular
bellen	to bark
sich **benehmen**	to behave
benutzen	to use

das **Benzin**	petrol
bequem	comfortable
der **Berg** (e)	mountain
der **Bericht** (e)	report
berichten	to report
der **Beruf** (e)	profession
die **Berufsschule** (n)	vocational school
berühmt	famous
beschäftigt	busy
beschließen	to decide
beschreiben	to describe
die **Beschreibung** (en)	description
sich **beschweren**	to complain
besetzt	occupied
besichtigen	to view
besonders	especially
besorgen	to get
besser	better
das **Besteck**	cutlery
bestehen	to pass (exams)
bestellen	to order (a meal, etc)
bestimmt	certain, definite
der **Besuch** (e)	visit
besuchen	to visit
betreten	to enter
betrunken	drunk
das **Bett** (en)	bed
die **Bettdecke** (n)	blanket
die **Bettwäsche**	bedclothes
die **Bevölkerung** (en)	population
(sich) **bewegen**	to move
der **Beweis** (e)	proof

bewölkt	cloudy
bewundern	to admire
bezahlen	to pay
die **Bibliothek** (en)	library
die **Biene** (n)	bee
das **Bier**	beer
bieten	to offer
das **Bild** (er)	picture
billig	cheap
binden	to tie
die **Biologie**	biology
die **Birne** (n)	pear
Bis bald!	See you soon!
Bis später!	See you later!
ein **bißchen**	a little
bitte (schön)	please; you're welcome
bitten	to ask for
die **Blaskapelle** (n)	brass band
blaß	pale
das **Blatt** (¨er)	leaf
blau	blue
bleiben	to stay
der **Bleistift** (e)	pencil
der **Blick** (e)	look
blind	blind
der **Blitz**	lightning
die **Blockflöte** (n)	recorder
blöd	stupid
der **Blödsinn**	nonsense
blond	blond
die **Blume** (n)	flower

der **Blumenkohl**	cauliflower
die **Bluse** (n)	blouse
das **Blut**	blood
bluten	to bleed
die **Bockwurst** (¨e)	sausage
der **Boden** (¨)	ground
der **Bodensee**	Lake Constance
die **Bohne** (n)	bean
das **Bonbon** (s)	sweet
das **Boot** (e)	boat
borgen	to borrow
böse	angry
braten	to roast
das **Brathähnchen** (-)	roast chicken
die **Bratkartoffel** (n)	roast potato
die **Bratwurst** (¨e)	sausage
brauchen	to need
braun	brown
brechen	to break
die **BRD**	West Germany
breit	wide
die **Bremse** (n)	brake
bremsen	to brake
brennen	to burn
das **Brett** (er)	board
der **Brief** (e)	letter
der **Brieffreund** (e)	pen-friend
der **Briefkasten** (¨)	letter-box
die **Briefmarke** (n)	stamp
die **Brieftasche** (n)	wallet
der **Briefträger** (-)	postman
die **Brille** (n)	spectacles

bringen	to bring
die **Broschüre** (n)	brochure
das **Brot** (e)	bread; loaf
das **Brötchen** (-)	bread roll
die **Brücke** (n)	bridge
der **Bruder** (¨)	brother
die **Brust** (¨e)	chest; breast
das **Buch** (¨er)	book
buchen	to book
buchstabieren	to spell
bügeln	to iron
die **Bühne** (n)	stage
der **Bungalow** (s)	bungalow
bunt	colourful
die **Burg** (en)	castle
der **Bürgermeister** (-)	mayor
der **Bürgersteig** (e)	pavement
das **Büro** (s)	office
die **Bürste** (n)	brush
bürsten	to brush
der **Bus** (se)	bus
der **Büstenhalter** (-)	bra
die **Butter**	butter
das **Butterbrot** (e)	bread and butter

das **Café** (s)	café
der **Campingplatz** (¨e)	camp-site
der **Champignon** (s)	mushroom
der **Chef** (s)	boss
die **Chemie**	chemistry
die **Chips**	crisps
die **Cola**	Coca-Cola
der **Computer** (-)	computer

ABC**D**EFGHIJKLMNOPQRSTUVWXYZ

da	there; as
das **Dach** (¨er)	roof
der **Dachboden** (¨)	attic
damals	at that time
die **Dame** (n)	lady
Damen	Ladies
der **Dampfer** (-)	steamship
dankbar	grateful
danke (schön)	thank you (very much)
danken	to thank
dann	then
das geht	that's alright
dasselbe	the same
das **Datum** (Daten)	date

dauern	to last
der **Daumen** (-)	thumb
die **DDR**	East Germany
die **Decke** (n)	ceiling
decken	to cover
denken	to think
das **Denkmal** (¨er)	monument
deutlich	clear(ly)
die **Deutsche** Bundesbahn	German Railways
Deutschland/Deutscher	Germany/German
deutsch	German
das **Dia** (s)	slide (film)
dick	fat; thick
der **Dieb** (e)	thief
dienen	to serve
der **Dienst** (e)	service
das **Ding** (e)	thing
direkt	direct
der **Direktor** (en)	headmaster
die **Diskothek** (en)	discotheque
doch	yet
der **Dom** (e)	cathedral
die **Donau**	Danube
der **Donner**	thunder
doof	stupid
das **Doppelhaus** (¨er)	semi-detached house
das **Doppelzimmer** (-)	double room
das **Dorf** (¨er)	village
dort	there
die **Dose** (n)	tin
der **Dosenöffner** (-)	tin-opener
dreckig	dirty

die **Drogerie** (n)	chemist's shop
drohen	to threaten
drüben	over there
drücken	to push
dumm	stupid
dunkel	dark
dünn	thin
durcheinander	in confusion
der **Durchfall**	diarrhoea
durchfallen*	to fail
der **Durchgangsverkehr**	through traffic
dürfen	to be allowed
der **Durst**	thirst
die **Dusche**	shower
sich **duschen**	to have a shower
das **Dutzend** (e)	dozen
der **D-Zug** (¨-e)	through train

ABCDEFGHIJKLMNOPQRSTUVWXYZ

echt	genuine
die **Ecke** (n)	corner
das **Ehepaar** (e)	married couple
ehrlich	honest
das **Ei** (er)	egg

eigen	own
eilen	to hurry
der **Eilzug** (¨e)	express train
die **Einbahnstraße** (n)	one-way street
der **Einbrecher** (-)	burglar
einfach	simple
die **Einfahrt** (en)	entrance
das **Einfamilienhaus** (¨er)	detached house
der **Eingang** (¨e)	entrance
einige	some
Einkäufe machen	to do the shopping
einkaufen*	to shop
der **Einkaufskorb** (¨e)	shopping basket
der **Einkaufswagen** (-)	shopping trolley
das **Einkaufszentrum** (en)	shopping centre
einladen*	to invite
die **Einladung** (en)	invitation
einlösen*	to change (cheques)
einmal	once
einordnen*	to arrange in order
einpacken*	to pack up
einreiben*	to rub in
einreichen*	to hand in
einschalten*	to switch on
einschlafen*	to fall asleep
einschließlich	inclusive
einsteigen*	to get on
der **Einstieg** (e)	entrance (bus, etc)
der **Eintopf** (¨e)	stew
der **Eintritt** (e)	entrance
die **Eintrittskarte** (n)	admission ticket
einverstanden	agreed

einwerfen*	to post
der **Einwohner** (-)	inhabitant
der **Einwurf** (¨-e)	slot
die **Einzelkarte** (n)	single ticket
das **Einzelkind** (er)	only child
das **Einzelzimmer** (-)	single room
das **Eis**	ice; ice-cream
der **Eisbecher** (-)	bowl of ice-cream
die **Eisenbahn**	railway
der **Elefant** (en)	elephant
der **Elektriker** (-)	electrician
elektrisch	electric
der **Elektroherd** (e)	electric cooker
die **Eltern** (pl.)	parents
der **Empfang** (¨-e)	reception
die **Empfangsdame** (n)	receptionist
empfehlen	to recommend
das **Ende** (n)	end
endlich	at last
das **Endspiel** (e)	final (sport)
eng	narrow; tight
England/Engländer	England/Englishman
englisch	English
der **Enkel** (-)	grandson
entdecken	to discover
die **Ente** (n)	duck
die **Entfernung** (en)	distance
sich **entscheiden**	to decide
entschuldigen	to excuse
sich **entschuldigen**	to apologize
Entschuldigung!	Excuse me!

	entwerten	to stamp (ticket)
die	**Erbse** (n)	pea
die	**Erdbeere** (n)	strawberry
die	**Erde**	earth
das	**Erdgeschoß**	ground floor
die	**Erdkunde**	geography
	erfahren	to find out
die	**Erfahrung** (en)	experience
der	**Erfolg** (e)	success
die	**Erfrischungen** (pl.)	refreshments
das	**Ergebnis** (se)	result
	erhalten	to receive
	erhältlich	available
sich	**erholen**	to recover
sich	**erinnern**	to remember
	erkältet sein	to have a cold
die	**Erkältung** (en)	cold (i.e. illness)
	erkennen	to recognize
	erklären	to explain
die	**Erklärung** (en)	explanation
sich	**erkundigen** nach	to inquire about
	erlauben	to allow
die	**Ermäßigung** (en)	reduction
	erreichen	to reach
	erscheinen	to appear
	erst um	not until
	erste Hilfe	first aid
	erwachen	to awake
der/die	**Erwachsene** (n)	adult (person)
	erzählen	to tell
	es gibt	there are
	es ist mir egal	it's all the same to me

es macht nichts	it doesn't matter
es tut mir leid	I am sorry
das **Essen**	food
essen	to eat
der **Essig**	vinegar
das **Eßzimmer** (-)	dining-room
die **Etage** (n)	storey
Europa/Europäer	Europe/European
europäisch	European
etwa	approximately
etwas	something
evangelisch	Protestant
die **E(W)G**	E(E)C

ABCDEFGHIJKLMNOPQRSTUVWXYZ

die **Fabrik** (en)	factory
das **Fach** (¨er)	subject
die **Fachhochschule** (n)	technical high school
der **Fahrausweis** (e)	ticket
die **Fähre** (n)	ferry
fahren	to go; to drive
der **Fahrer** (-)	driver
die **Fahrkarte** (n)	ticket
der **Fahrplan** (¨e)	timetable (e.g. railway)

der **Fahrpreis** (e)	fare
das **Fahrrad** (¨er)	bicycle
× der **Fahrschein** (e)	ticket
der **Fahrstuhl** (¨e)	lift
die **Fahrt** (en)	journey
das **Fahrzeug** (e)	vehicle
der **Fall** (¨e)	fall; case
fallen	to fall
fallenlassen	to drop
falsch	wrong
die **Familie** (n)	family
der **Familienname** (n)	surname
fangen	to catch
die **Farbe** (n)	colour
der **Fasching**	carnival
fast	almost
faul	lazy
der **Federball**	badminton
das **Federbett** (en)	duvet
fehlen	to be missing
der **Fehler** (-)	mistake
der **Feierabend**	closing-time; end of working day
der **Feiertag** (e)	public holiday
das **Feld** (er)	field
das **Fenster** (-)	window
die **Ferien** (pl.)	holidays
das **Ferngespräch** (e)	trunk-call
der **Fernsehapparat** (e)	television set
das **Fernsehen**	television
fernsehen*	to watch television
der **Fernseher** (-)	television set

der **Fernsprecher** (-) — telephone
fertig — ready; finished
das **Fest** (e) — party
festhalten* — to hold tight
feucht — damp
das **Feuer** (-) — fire
Feuer haben — to have a light
der **Feuerlöscher** (-) — fire extinguisher
die **Feuerwehr** — fire brigade
der **Feuerwehrwagen** (-) — fire engine
das **Feuerzeug** (e) — cigarette lighter
Fieber haben — to have a temperature
der **Film** (e) — film
der **Filzstift** (e) — felt-tip pen
finden — to find
der **Finger** — finger
die **Firma** (..en) — firm
der **Fisch** (e) — fish
flach — flat
die **Flasche** (n) — bottle
der **Flaschenöffner** (-) — bottle-opener
das **Fleisch** — meat
fleißig — hard-working
die **Fliege** (n) — fly
fliegen — to fly
fließen — to flow
fließend — fluent
die **Flöte** (n) — flute
der **Flug** (¨e) — flight
der **Flughafen** (¨) — airport
das **Flugzeug** (e) — aeroplane

der **Flur** (e)	hall
der **Fluß** (¨e)	river
folgen	to follow
die **Forelle** (n)	trout
das **Formular** (e)	form
der **Forst** (e)	forest
das **Foto** (s)	photograph
der **Fortschritt** (e)	progress
der **Fotoapparat** (e)	camera
fotografieren	to photograph
die **Frage** (n)	question
eine **Frage** stellen	to ask a question
fragen	to ask
Frankreich/Franzose	France/Frenchman
französisch	French
die **Frau** (en)	woman
Frau	Mrs
das **Fräulein** (-)	young lady
Fräulein	Miss
frech	cheeky
frei	free
das **Freibad** (¨er)	open-air swimming pool
freihalten*	to keep free
die **Freizeit**	leisure time
das **Fremdenzimmer** (-)	room to let
die **Fremdsprache** (n)	foreign language
fressen	(of animals) to eat
sich **freuen**	to be pleased
sich **freuen auf**	to look forward to
der **Freund** (e)	friend
freundlich	friendly

• der **Friede** (n) •	peace
der **Friedhof** (¨e)	cemetery
frieren	to freeze
die **Frikadelle** (n)	rissole
frisch	fresh
der **Friseur** (e)	hairdresser
froh	glad
fröhlich	merry
die **Frucht** (¨e)	fruit
früh	early
das **Frühstück**	breakfast
frühstücken	to breakfast
fühlen	to feel
führen	to lead
der **Führer** (-)	guide
der **Führerschein** (e)	driving licence
die **Führung** (en)	conduct; behaviour
füllen	to fill
der **Füller** (-)	fountain pen
das **Fundbüro** (s)	lost-property office
funktionieren	to function
furchtbar	terrible
der **Fuß** (¨e)	foot
der **Fußball** (¨e)	football
der **Fußballplatz** (¨e)	football ground
der **Fußboden** (¨)	floor
der **Fußgänger** (-)	pedestrian
der **Fußgängerzone** (n)	pedestrian precinct
füttern	to feed (animals)

die **Gabel** (n)	fork
der **Gang** (¨e)	corridor
die **Gans** (¨e)	goose
ganz	whole; quite
gar nicht	not at all
die **Garderobe** (n)	cloakroom
die **Garage** (n)	garage
der **Garten** (¨)	garden
Gas geben	to accelerate
der **Gast** (¨e)	guest
der **Gastgeber** (-)	host
das **Gasthaus** (¨er)	public house •
der **Gasthof** (¨e)	hotel
die **Gaststätte** (n)	restaurant •
das **Gebäude** (-)	building
geben	to give
das **Gebiet** (e)	region
das **Gebirge**	mountains
geboren	born
gebrauchen	to use
die **Gebrauchsanweisungen**	instructions for use
die **Gebühr** (en)	fee
die **Geburt** (en)	birth
das **Geburtsdatum** (..daten)	date of birth
der **Geburtsort** (e)	place of birth
der **Geburtstag** (e)	birthday
die **Gefahr** (en)	danger
gefährlich	dangerous
gefallen	to please
die **Gegend** (en)	area
das **Gegenteil** (e)	opposite
der **Gehalt** (e)	salary

gehen	to go
gehören	to belong
die **Geige** (n)	violin
gelb	yellow
das **Geld** (er)	money
die **Geldstrafe** (n)	fine
die **Gelegenheit** (en)	opportunity
gemischt	mixed
das **Gemüse**	vegetables
gemütlich	cosy
genau	exact(ly)
genug	enough
genügen	to be enough
geöffnet	open
die **Geographie**	geography
das **Gepäck**	luggage
die **Gepäckaufbewahrung**	left-luggage office
das **Gepäcknetz** (e)	luggage-rack
der **Gepäckträger** (-)	porter
gerade	just; straight
geradeaus	straight ahead
das **Gericht** (e)	court
gern haben	to like
die **Gesamtschule** (n)	comprehensive school
das **Geschäft** (e)	shop
der **Geschäftsmann** (..leute)	businessman
die **Geschäftszeiten**	office hours, business hours
geschehen	to happen
das **Geschenk** (e)	present
die **Geschichte** (n)	story; history

geschieden	separated
das **Geschirr**	crockery
das **Geschlecht** (er)	sex; gender
geschlossen	closed
der **Geschmack** (¨-e)	taste
die **Geschwister** (pl.)	brothers and sisters
die **Geschwindigkeit** (en)	speed
das **Gesicht** (er)	face
gesperrt	blocked
das **Gespräch** (e)	conversation
gestattet	allowed
gestern	yesterday
gestreift	striped
gesund	healthy
die **Gesundheit**	health
Gesundheit!	Bless you!
das **Getränk** (e)	drink
die **Getränkekarte** (n)	list of drinks
getrennt	separate(ly)
das **Gewicht** (e)	weight
gewinnen	to win
gewiß	certain(ly)
das **Gewitter** (-)	thunder storm
die **Gewohnheit** (en)	habit
gewöhnlich	usual(ly)
der **Gipfel** (-)	summit
der **Gips**	plaster (of Paris)
die **Gitarre** (n)	guitar
das **Glas** (¨-er)	glass
glatt	smooth
die **Glatze** (n)	bald head
glauben	to think; to believe

gleich	same; at once
gleichfalls	likewise
das **Gleis** (e)	platform
das **Glück**	luck, happiness
glücklich	happy
der **Glückwunsch** (¨e)	congratulations
das **Gold**	gold
der **Gott** (¨er)	God
der **Gottesdienst** (e)	church service
der **Grad** (e)	degree
das **Gramm** (e)	gram(me)
das **Gras**	grass
gratulieren	to congratulate
grau	grey
die **Grenze** (n)	border
grillen	to barbecue
die **Grippe**	influenza
groß	big; great
großartig	great
die **Großeltern** (pl.)	grandparents
die **Großmutter** (¨)	grandmother
die **Großstadt** (¨e)	city
der **Großvater** (¨)	grandfather
großzügig	generous
die **Grundschule** (n)	primary school
die **Gruppe** (n)	group
der **Gruß** (¨e)	greeting
grüß Gott!	Hello!
grüßen	to greet
grün	green
gucken	to look
gültig	valid

der **Gummi**	rubber
günstig	favourable
die **Gurke** (n)	cucumber
der **Gürtel** (-)	belt
gut	good
gut gelaunt	in a good mood
gute Besserung!	Get well soon!
gute Nacht!	Good night!
gute Reise!	Have a good journey!
guten Abend!	Good evening!
guten Morgen!	Good morning!
guten Tag!	Good day!
das **Gymnasium** (..en)	grammar school

ABCDEFGHIJKLMNOPQRSTUVWXYZ

das **Haar** (e)	hair
die **Haarbürste** (n)	hairbrush
der **Haartrockner** (-)	hair-dryer
haben	to have
der **Hafen** (¨)	harbour
der **Hagel**	hail
hageln	to hail
das **Hähnchen** (-)	chicken

halb	half
Halbpension	half-board
die **Hälfte** (n)	half
das **Hallenbad** (¨er)	indoor swimming-pool
der **Hals** (¨e)	throat
halten	to hold; to stop
die **Haltestelle** (n)	stop
der **Hamster** (-)	hamster
die **Hand** (¨e)	hand
die **Handarbeit** (en)	handicraft
die **Handlung** (en)	action
der **Handschuh** (e)	glove
die **Handtasche** (n)	handbag
das **Handtuch** (¨er)	towel
hart	hard
häßlich	ugly
der **Haufen** (-)	pile
der **Hauptbahnhof** (¨e)	main station
die **Hauptschule** (n)	secondary modern school
die **Hauptstadt** (¨e)	capital city
die **Hauptstraße** (n)	main street
das **Haus** (¨er)	house
die **Hausaufgabe** (n)	homework
die **Hausfrau** (en)	housewife
der **Haushalt** (e)	household
der **Hausmeister** (-)	caretaker
die **Hausnummer** (n)	house number
das **Haustier** (e)	pet
das **Heft** (e)	exercise book
das **Heftpflaster** (-)	sticking-plaster

der **Heilige Abend**	Christmas Eve
die **Heimat**	homeland
das **Heimweh**	homesickness
heiraten	to marry
heiß	hot
heißen	to be called
heiter	bright
heizen	to heat
die **Heizung** (en)	heating
helfen	to help
hell	light
das **Hemd** (en)	shirt
die **Herbergsmutter** (¨-)	hostel warden (*f*)
der **Herbergsvater** (¨-)	hostel warden (*m*)
der **Herd** (e)	cooker
der **Herr** (en)	gentleman
Herr ...	Mr
Herr Ober!	Waiter!
Herren	Gentlemen
die **Herrenkonfektion** (en)	menswear
die **Herrenmode** (n)	men's fashion
herrlich	magnificent
das **Herz** (en)	heart
herzlichen Glückwunsch!	Congratulations!
heute	today
hier	here
die **Hilfe** (n)	help
die **Himbeere** (n)	raspberry
der **Himmel** (-)	sky; heaven
hin und zurück	there and back
hinauslehnen*	to lean out
sich **hinlegen***	to lie down

sich **hinsetzen***	to sit down
hinten	at the back
die **Hitze**	heat
das **Hobby** (s)	hobby
hoch	high
hochachtungsvoll	yours faithfully
das **Hochhaus** (¨er)	skyscraper
die **Hochschule** (n)	college
der **Hochsprung**	high jump
die **Höchstgeschwindigkeit**	top speed
die **Hochzeit** (en)	wedding
der **Hof** (¨e)	yard
hoffen	to hope
hoffentlich	I hope
höflich	polite
holen	to fetch
Holland/Holländer	Holland/Dutchman
holländisch	Dutch
das **Holz** (¨er)	wood (i.e. material)
der **Honig**	honey
hören	to hear
der **Hörer** (-)	telephone receiver
die **Hose** (n)	trousers
das **Hotel** (s)	hotel
hübsch	pretty
der **Hubschrauber** (-)	helicopter
der **Hügel** (-)	hill
das **Huhn** (¨er)	chicken
der **Hund** (e)	dog
der **Hunger**	hunger
hungrig	hungry
husten	to cough

der **Hut** (¨-er)	hat
die **Hütte** (n)	hut

ABCDEFGH**I**JKLMNOPQRSTUVWXYZ

Ich hätte gern	I would like
Ich möchte	I would like
die **Idee** (n)	idea
die **Illustrierte** (n)	magazine
im Freien	in the open air
der **Imbiß** (e)	snack
die **Imbißstube** (n)	snack-bar
immer	always
inbegriffen	included
die **Industrie** (n)	industry
die **Informatik**	computer studies
das **Informationsbüro** (s)	information office
der **Ingenieur** (e)	engineer
inklusive	inclusive
das **Insekt** (e)	insect
die **Insel** (n)	island
das **Instrument** (e)	instrument
intelligent	intelligent
interessant	interesting
das **Interesse**	interest

sich **interessieren für**	to be interested in
irgendwas	something or other
irisch	Irish
Irland/Irländer	Ireland/Irishman
Italien/Italiener	Italy/Italian
italienisch	Italian

ABCDEFGHIJKLMNOPQRSTUVWXYZ

ja	yes
die **Jacke** (n)	jacket
das **Jahr** (e)	year
die **Jahreszeit** (en)	season
das **Jahrhundert** (e)	century
jährlich	annual
jed-	every
jetzt	now
das **Joghurt**	yogurt
die **Jugend**	youth
die **Jugendherberge** (n)	youth hostel
der **Jugendklub** (s)	youth club
• der/die **Jugendliche** (n)	young person
jung	young
der **Junge** (n)	boy

der **Kaffee**	coffee
die **Kaffeekanne** (n)	coffee-pot
der **Käfig** (e)	cage
der **Kakao**	cocoa
das **Kalbfleisch**	veal
kalt	cold
die **Kälte**	cold
die **Kalte** Platte	cold buffet
der **Kamin** (e)	fireplace
der **Kamm** (¨-e)	comb
kämmen	to comb
der **Kanal** (¨-e)	canal; channel
das **Kaninchen** (-)	rabbit
das **Kännchen** (-)	pot
die **Kapelle** (n)	chapel; band
kapieren	to understand
kaputt	broken
kariert	checked
die **Karte** (n)	card
die **Kartoffel** (n)	potato
der **Kartoffelbrei**	mashed potato
der **Kartoffelsalat**	potato salad
der **Käse**	cheese
die **Kasse** (n)	cash desk
der **Kassenzettel** (-)	receipt
die **Kassette** (n)	cassette
der **Kassettenrekorder** (-)	cassette recorder
der **Kassierer** (-)	cashier
einen **Kater** haben	to have a hangover
die **Katze** (n)	cat
kauen	to chew
kaufen	to buy

das **Kaufhaus** (¨er)	department store
der **Kaufmann** (..leute)	merchant
der **Kaugummi**	chewing-gum
kaum	hardly
kegeln	to play skittles
der **Keks** (e)	biscuit
der **Keller** (-)	cellar
der **Kellner** (-)	waiter
kennen	to know
kennenlernen	to get to know
die **Kerze** (n)	candle
die **Kette** (n)	chain
das **Kilo** (s)	kilogram(me)
das **Kind** (er)	child
das **Kino** (s)	cinema
der **Kiosk** (e)	kiosk
die **Kirche** (n)	church
die **Kirsche** (n)	cherry
das **Kissen** (-)	cushion
klappen	to succeed; to fold
der **Klappstuhl** (¨e)	folding chair
der **Klapptisch** (e)	folding table
klar	clear
Klasse!	Great!
die **Klasse** (n)	class
die **Klassenarbeit** (en)	class test
die **Klassenfahrt** (en)	class trip
der **Klassenkamerad** (en)	classmate
der **Klassenlehrer** (-)	form teacher
der **Klassensprecher** (-)	form captain
das **Klassenzimmer** (-)	classroom
klassisch	classical

klauen	to pinch (i.e. steal)
das **Klavier** (e)	piano
kleben	to stick
das **Kleid** (er)	dress
die **Kleider** (pl.)	clothes
der **Kleiderschrank** (¨e)	wardrobe
die **Kleidung**	clothing
klein	small; little
das **Kleingeld**	change (i.e. money)
klettern	to climb
das **Klima**	climate
klingeln	to ring
die **Klinik** (en)	clinic
das **Klo** (s)	toilet
klopfen	to knock
klug	clever
die **Kneipe** (n)	pub
das **Knie** (n)	knee
der **Knödel** (-)	dumpling
der **Knopf** (¨e)	button
der **Koch** (¨e)	cook
kochen	to cook
der **Koffer** (-)	suitcase
der **Kofferkuli** (s)	luggage trolley
der **Kofferraum** (¨e)	boot (of car)
der **Kohl**	cabbage
die **Kohle**	coal
Köln	Cologne
komisch	funny
kommen	to come
die **Komödie** (n)	comedy
kompliziert	complicated

das **Kompott**	stewed fruit
die **Konditorei** (en)	confectioner's shop
können	to be able
kontrollieren	to check
das **Konzert** (e)	concert
der **Kopf** (¨e)	head
das **Kopfkissen** (-)	pillow
der **Kopfsalat**	lettuce
der **Korb** (¨e)	basket
der **Körper** (-)	body
körperbehindert	disabled
korrigieren	to correct
kostbar	costly
kosten	to cost
kostenlos	free of charge
das **Kostüm** (e)	costume
das **Kotelett** (en)	cutlet
krank	sick, ill
das **Krankenhaus** (¨er)	hospital
die **Krankenkasse** (n)	health insurance
der **Krankenschein** (e)	medical certificate
die **Krankenschwester** (n)	nurse
der **Krankenwagen** (-)	ambulance
die **Krankheit** (en)	illness
die **Krawatte** (n)	tie
die **Kreide**	chalk
der **Kreis** (e)	circle
die **Kreuzung** (en)	crossroads
der **Krieg** (e)	war
kriegen	to get
der **Krimi** (s)	thriller
die **Küche** (n)	kitchen

der **Kuchen** (-)	cake
die **Kuckucksuhr** (en)	cuckoo clock
der **Kugelschreiber** (-)	ballpoint pen
die **Kuh** (¨e)	cow
kühl	cool
der **Kühlschrank** (¨e)	refrigerator
der **Kuli** (s)	ballpoint pen
der **Kunde** (n)	customer
die **Kunst** (¨e)	art
der **Künstler** (-)	artist
der **Kunststoff** (e)	synthetic material
die **Kur** (en)	cure
der **Kurort** (e)	health resort
der **Kurs** (e)	exchange rate
kurz	short
die **Kusine** (n)	cousin
die **Küste** (n)	coast

ABCDEFGHIJK**L**MNOPQRSTUVWXYZ

das **Labor** (e)	laboratory
lachen	to laugh
lächeln	to smile
der **Laden** (¨)	shop

die **Lage** (n)	situation
das **Lamm** (¨-er)	lamb
die **Lampe** (n)	lamp
das **Land** (¨-er)	country
die **Landkarte** (n)	map
die **Landschaft** (en)	countryside
lang	long
lange	for a long time
langsam	slow(ly)
die **Langspielplatte** (n)	LP record
sich **langweilen**	to be bored
langweilig	boring
der **Lappen** (-)	cloth
der **Lärm**	noise
lassen	to let
der **Lastwagen** (-)	lorry
Latein	Latin
laufen	to run
laut	loud
läuten	to ring
leben	to live
die **Lebensgefahr** (en)	danger to life
die **Lebensmittel** (pl.)	groceries
das **Lebensmittelgeschäft**	grocer's shop
die **Leberwurst** (¨-e)	liver sausage
lebhaft	lively
lecker	delicious
das **Leder**	leather
ledig	single (unmarried)
leer	empty
leermachen*	to empty
die **Leerung** (en)	postal collection

legen	to put
die **Lehre** (n)	apprenticeship
der **Lehrer** (-)	teacher
das **Lehrerzimmer** (-)	staffroom
der **Lehrling** (e)	apprentice
leicht	easy
die **Leichtathletik**	athletics
leiden	to bear
leider	unfortunately
leihen	to lend
leise	quiet(ly)
die **Leistung** (en)	achievement
lernen	to learn
lesen	to read
letzt	last
die **Leute** (pl.)	people
das **Licht** (er)	light
lieben	to love
der **Liebling**	favourite
das **Lieblingsfach** (¨er)	favourite subject
das **Lied** (er)	song
liefern	to deliver
der **Lieferwagen** (-)	delivery van
liegen	to lie
der **Liegewagen** (-)	couchette
die **Limonade**	lemonade
das **Lineal** (e)	ruler
link	left
die **Liste** (n)	list
das **Liter** (-)	litre
der **LKW**	lorry
loben	to praise

der **Löffel** (-)	spoon
der **Lohn** (¨e)	wage
lösen	to buy (ticket)
der **Löwe** (n)	lion
die **Luft**	air
die **Luftmatraze** (n)	air-bed
die **Luftpost**	airmail
Lust haben	to want to
lustig	funny

ABCDEFGHIJKLMNOPQRSTUVWXYZ

machen	to make; to do
Mach's gut!	See you!
das **Mädchen** (-)	girl
der **Magen** (-)	stomach
mähen	to mow
die **Mahlzeit** (en)	meal
das **Mal** (e)	time (occasion)
malen	to paint
man	one (pronoun)
manchmal	sometimes
mangelhaft	deficient
der **Mann** (¨er)	man
männlich	masculine

die **Mannschaft** (en)	team
der **Mantel** (¨-)	coat
die **Mappe** (n)	briefcase
die **Margarine**	margarine
die **Marke** (n)	brand
der **Markt** (¨-e)	market
der **Marktplatz** (¨-e)	market-place
die **Marmelade**	jam
die **Maschine** (n)	machine
die **Mathe**	maths
der **Matrose** (n)	sailor
die **Mauer** (n)	wall
die **Maus** (¨-e)	mouse
der **Mechaniker** (-)	mechanic
das **Medikament** (e)	medicament
die **Medizin** (en)	medicine
das **Meer** (e)	sea
das **Meerschweinchen** (-)	guinea-pig
mehr	more
mehrere	several
das **Mehrwertsteuer**	VAT
die **Meile** (n)	mile
meinen	to think
die **Meinung** (en)	opinion
melden	to report
die **Menge** (n)	crowd
der **Mensch** (en)	person
die **Messe** (n)	trade fair
das **Messer** (-)	knife
der **Metzger** (-)	butcher
die **Metzgerei** (en)	butcher's shop
die **Miete** (n)	rent

mieten	to rent
die **Milch**	milk
mild	mild
das **Mineralwasser**	mineral water
die **Minute** (n)	minute
das **Mißverständnis** (se)	misunderstanding
das **Mitglied** (er)	member
der **Mittag**	midday
das **Mittagessen** (-)	midday meal
die **Mitte** (n)	middle
mitteilen*	to inform
das **Mittelmeer**	Mediterranean Sea
mitten in	in the middle of
die **Mitternacht**	midnight
das **Möbel**	furniture
möbliert	furnished
die **Mode** (n)	fashion
modern	modern
das **Mofa** (s)	moped
mogeln	to cheat
mögen	to like
möglich	possible
die **Möhre** (n)	carrot
das **Moment** (e)	moment
der **Monat** (e)	month
monatlich	monthly
der **Mond** (e)	moon
morgen	tomorrow
der **Morgen** (-)	morning
der **Motor** (en)	engine
das **Motorrad** (¨er)	motorbike
die **Mücke** (n)	midge

müde	tired
München	Munich
der **Mund** (¨er)	mouth
mündlich	oral(ly)
die **Münze** (n)	coin
das **Museum** (Museen)	museum
die **Musik**	music
der **Musiker** (-)	musician
müssen	must; to have to
die **Mutter** (¨)	mother
Mutti	Mum
die **Mütze** (n)	cap

ABCDEFGHIJKLM**N**OPQRSTUVWXYZ

der **Nachbar** (n)	neighbour
nachher	afterwards
der **Nachmittag** (e)	afternoon
der **Nachname** (n)	surname
die **Nachrichten** (pl.)	news
nachsitzen*	to be in detention
die **Nachspeise** (n)	sweet
nächst	next
die **Nacht** (¨e)	night
der **Nachtisch** (e)	sweet (final course)

der **Nachttisch** (e)	bedside table
die **Nadel** (n)	needle
in der **Nähe** von	near
nähen	to sew
der **Nahverkehrszug** (¨e)	local train
der **Name** (n)	name
der **Namenstag** (e)	name-day
die **Nase** (n)	nose
naß	wet
die **Natur**	nature
natürlich	natural(ly)
die **Naturwissenschaft** (en)	science
der **Nebel**	fog
nebenan	next-door
die **Nebenstraße** (n)	side street
neblig	foggy
der **Neffe** (n)	nephew
nehmen	to take
nein	no
nennen	to call (i.e. name)
nervös	nervous
nett	nice
das **Netz** (e)	net
neu	new
neugierig	curious
das **Neujahr**	New Year
neulich	recently
nicht	not
nicht mehr	no longer
die **Nichte** (n)	niece
der **Nichtraucher** (-)	non-smoker
nichts	nothing

nichts zu danken	don't mention it
nie	never
die **Niederlande/ Niederländer**	the Netherlands/ Dutchman
niederländisch	Dutch
der **Niederschlag** (¨-e)	precipitation (i.e. rain)
niemand	nobody
niesen	to sneeze
noch	still
noch einmal	once again
noch nicht	not yet
der **Norden**	north
die **Nordsee**	North See
Normal	three-star petrol
der **Notausgang** (¨-e)	emergency exit
der **Notdienst** (e)	emergency service
die **Note** (n)	mark (for school work)
das **Notizbuch** (¨-er)	notebook
der **Notruf** (e)	emergency call
null	nought
die **Nummer** (n)	number
nun	now
nur	only
nützlich	useful

oben	upstairs
das **Obergeschoß**	upper storey
die **Oberstufe**	sixth form
das **Obst**	fruit
der **Ofen** (¨-)	stove
offen	open
offensichtlich	obvious(ly)
öffentlich	public
öffnen	to open
die **Öffnungszeiten** (pl.)	opening hours
oft	often
das **Ohr** (en)	ear
das **Öl**	oil
die **Oma**	grandma
das **Omelett**	omelette
der **Onkel** (-)	uncle
der **Opa**	grandad
der **Orangensaft**	orange juice
das **Orchester** (-)	orchestra
die **Ordnung** (en)	order (i.e. behaviour)
organisieren	to organize
der **Ort** (e)	place
das **Ortsgespräch** (e)	local call
der **Osten**	east
Ostern	Easter
Österreich/Österreicher	Austria/Austrian
österreichisch	Austrian
die **Ostsee**	Baltic Sea

ein **paar**	a few
das **Paar** (e)	pair
das **Päckchen** (-)	packet
packen	to pack
die **Packung** (en)	packet
das **Paket** (e)	parcel
paniert	with breadcrumbs
die **Panne** (n)	breakdown (mechanical)
der **Pantoffel** (n)	slipper
das **Papier** (e)	paper
der **Park** (s)	park
parken	to park
das **Parkett**	stalls (i.e. cinema)
das **Parkhaus** (¨-er)	multi-storey car park
der **Parkplatz** (¨-e)	car park
der **Parkschein** (e)	parking-ticket
die **Parkuhr** (en)	parking-meter
Parkverbot	No Parking
das **Parterre**	ground floor
der **Partner** (-)	partner
der **Paß** (¨-e)	passport
der **Passagier** (e)	passenger
passen	to fit
passieren	to happen
die **Paßkontrolle** (n)	passport control
der **Patient** (en)	patient
die **Pause** (n)	pause; break-time
das **Pech**	bad luck
die **Pension** (en)	boarding-house
per Anhalter fahren	to hitchhike
die **Person** (en)	person

der **Personenzug** (¨-e)	passenger train
der **Pfad** (e)	path
der **Pfadfinder** (-)	boy scout
der **Pfeffer**	pepper
die **Pfeife** (n)	pipe
das **Pferd** (e)	horse
Pfingsten	Whitsun
der **Pfirsich** (e)	peach
die **Pflanze** (n)	plant
das **Pflaster** (-)	plaster
die **Pflaume** (n)	plum
pflegen	to take care of
die **Pflicht** (en)	duty
das **Pflichtfach** (¨-er)	compulsory subject
das **Pfund** (e)	pound
die **Physik**	physics
die **Pille** (n)	pill
der **Pilz** (e)	mushroom
der **PKW**	car
planmäßig	planned
die **Platte** (n)	record
der **Plattenspieler** (-)	record-player
der **Platz** (¨-e)	place; square
Platz machen	to make room
Platz nehmen	to take a seat
die **Platzkarte** (n)	ticket for reserved seat
plaudern	to chat
plötzlich	suddenly
der **Pokal** (e)	cup; trophy
die **Politik**	politics
die **Polizei**	police

die **Polizeiwache** (n)	police station
der **Polizist** (en)	policeman
die **Pommes** Frites	chips
die **Popmusik**	pop music
die **Portion** (en)	portion
das **Portmonnaie** (s)	purse
die **Post**	post office
das **Postamt** (⸚er)	post office
das **Poster** (-)	poster
die **Postkarte** (n)	postcard
die **Postleitzahl** (en)	postal code
das **Postwertzeichen** (-)	postage stamp
die **Praline** (n)	chocolate (sweet)
der **Preis** (e)	price; prize
preiswert	cheap
Prima!	Great!
pro	per
probieren	to try (i.e. taste)
das **Problem** (e)	problem
der **Profi** (s)	professional
das **Programm** (e)	programme
das **Prospekt** (e)	prospectus
Prost!	Cheers!
protestieren	to protest
prüfen	to test
die **Prüfung** (en)	test; examination
der **Pulli** (s)	pullover
der **Pullover** (-)	pullover
das **Pult** (e)	desk
der **Punkt** (e)	point
pünktlich	punctual
die **Puppe** (n)	doll
putzen	to clean

die **Qualität** (en)	quality
der **Quatsch**	nonsense
Quer ...	cross ...
die **Quittung** (en)	receipt

ABCDEFGHIJKLMNOPQRSTUVWXYZ

das **Rad** (¨-er)	wheel; bike
radfahren*	to cycle
der **Radfahrer** (-)	cyclist
der **Radiergummi** (s)	rubber (eraser)
das **Radio** (s)	radio
der **Rang** (¨-e)	rank
der **Rasen** (-)	lawn
der **Rasierapparat** (e)	shaver
sich **rasieren**	to shave (oneself)
die **Raststätte** (n)	service station
raten	to guess; to advise
das **Rathaus** (¨-er)	town hall
rauchen	to smoke
der **Raucher** (-)	smoker
der **Raum** (¨-e)	room
die **Realschule** (n)	secondary school
rechnen	to reckon; to calculate

der **Rechner** (-)	calculator
die **Rechnung** (en)	bill
recht	right
recht haben	to be right
reden	to talk
das **Regal** (e)	shelf
regelmäßig	regular(ly)
der **Regen**	rain
der **Regenmantel** (¨-)	raincoat
der **Regenschirm** (e)	umbrella
regnen	to rain
regnerisch	rainy
reiben	to rub
reich	rich
reichen	to pass (i.e. hand over)
der **Reifen** (-)	tyre
der **Reifendruck**	tyre pressure
die **Reifenpanne** (n)	burst tyre
die **Reihe** (n)	row (of seats, etc)
das **Reihenhaus** (¨-er)	terraced house
der **Reis**	rice
die **Reise** (n)	journey
die **Reiseauskunft** (¨-e)	travel information
das **Reisebüro** (s)	travel agent's
der **Reisebus** (se)	coach
der **Reiseführer** (-)	guide-book
der **Reiseleiter** (-)	guide
reisen	to travel
der/die **Reisende** (n)	traveller
der **Reisescheck** (s)	traveller's cheque
reiten	to ride

die **Reklame** (n)	advertisement
die **Religion** (en)	religion
rennen	to run
der **Rentner** (-)	pensioner
die **Reparatur** (en)	repair
reparieren	to repair
reservieren	to reserve
die **Reservierung** (en)	reservation
das **Restaurant** (s)	restaurant
retten	to save
das **Rezept** (e)	recipe
der **Rhein**	Rhine
richtig	correct
die **Richtung** (en)	direction
riechen	to smell
das **Rindfleisch**	beef
der **Ring** (e)	ring
der **Rock** (¨e)	skirt
der **Roller** (-)	scooter
der **Rollschuh** (e)	roller-skate
die **Rolltreppe** (n)	escalator
der **Roman** (e)	novel
rosa	pink
rot	red
der **Rotwein**	red wine
der **Rücken** (-)	back
die **Rückfahrkarte** (n)	return ticket
die **Rückfahrt** (en)	return journey
der **Rucksack** (¨e)	rucksack
das **Ruderboot** (e)	rowing-boat
rudern	to row
rufen	to call

die **Ruhe** (n)	calm
Ruhe!	Quiet!
der **Ruhetag** (e)	closing-day
ruhig	calm
das **Rührei** (er)	scrambled egg
die **Ruine** (n)	ruin
rund	round
die **Rundfahrt** (en)	circular tour
der **Rundfunk**	broadcasting

ABCDEFGHIJKLMNOPQR**S**TUVWXYZ

die **S-Bahn**	urban railway
der **Saal** (Säle)	hall
die **Sache** (n)	thing
der **Saft** (¨e)	juice
sagen	to say
die **Sahne**	cream
die **Saison** (s)	season (football, etc)
der **Salat** (e)	salad
das **Salz**	salt
die **Salzkartoffel** (n)	boiled potato
sammeln	to collect
die **Sammlung** (en)	collection
der **Sand**	sand

die **Sandale** (n)	sandal
der **Sänger** (-)	singer
satt	full (after meal)
sauber	clean
sauber machen	to clean
sauer	sour
das **Schach**	chess
die **Schachtel** (n)	box
Schade!	Pity!
das **Schaf** (e)	sheep
der **Schaffner** (-)	conductor
der **Schal** (s)	scarf
die **Schale** (n)	bowl
schälen	to peel
die **Schallplatte** (n)	record
der **Schalter** (-)	counter
scharf	sharp
der **Schatten** (-)	shadow
schauen	to look
der **Schauer** (-)	shower (rain, etc)
das **Schaufenster** (-)	shop window
das **Schauspiel** (e)	play
der **Schauspieler** (-)	actor
der **Scheck** (s)	cheque
die **Scheckkarte** (n)	cheque card
die **Scheibe** (n)	slice; pane
der **Schein** (e)	note (i.e. banknote)
scheinen	to shine; to seem
der **Scheinwerfer** (-)	headlamp
schellen	to ring
schenken	to present; to give
schick	smart

schicken	to send
schief	sloping
schießen	to shoot
das **Schiff** (e)	ship
das **Schild** (er)	sign
die **Schildkröte** (n)	tortoise
der **Schinken** (-)	ham
der **Schlafanzug** (¨e)	pyjamas
schlafen	to sleep
der **Schlafsack** (¨e)	sleeping bag
der **Schlafwagen** (-)	sleeping car
das **Schlafzimmer** (-)	bedroom
schlagen	to hit
der **Schläger** (-)	bat (e.g. cricket)
die **Schlagsahne**	whipped cream
das **Schlagzeug**	percussion
die **Schlange** (n)	snake; queue
schlank	slim
schlecht	bad
schlecht gelaunt	in a bad mood
schließen	to close
das **Schließfach** (¨er)	locker
schließlich	finally
schlimm	bad
der **Schlips** (e)	tie
der **Schlittschuh** (e)	skate
das **Schloß** (¨er)	castle
schlucken	to swallow
der **Schluß** (¨e)	finish
der **Schlüssel** (-)	key
schmal	narrow
schmecken	to taste

schmerzen	to hurt
der **Schmuck**	jewellery
schmutzig	dirty
der **Schnee**	snow
schneiden	to cut
schneien	to snow
schnell	quick; fast
der **Schnellimbiß** (e)	snack-bar
die **Schnellreinigung** (en)	express cleaners
der **Schnellzug** (¨e)	express train
das **Schnitzel** (-)	cutlet
der **Schnupfen** (-)	cold (i.e. illness)
der **Schnurrbart** (¨e)	moustache
die **Schokolade**	chocolate
schon	already
schön	beautiful
Schottland/Schotte	Scotland/Scot, Scotsman
schottisch	Scots, Scottish
der **Schrank** (¨e)	cupboard
schrecklich	terrible
schreiben	to write
die **Schreibmaschine** (n)	typewriter
das **Schreibpapier**	writing paper
die **Schreibwaren**	stationery
die **Schreibwarenhandlung**	stationer's
schreien	to shout
schriftlich	in writing
schüchtern	shy
der **Schuh** (e)	shoe
die **Schule** (n)	school
der **Schüler** (-)	schoolboy

die **Schülermitverwaltung**	school council
der **Schulhof** (¨e)	schoolyard
die **Schultasche** (n)	school-bag
die **Schulter** (n)	shoulder
die **Schüssel** (n)	dish
schütteln	to shake
schützen	to protect
schwach	weak
der **Schwager** (-)	brother-in-law
der **Schwamm** (¨e)	sponge
schwänzen	to play truant
schwarz	black
schwarzfahren*	to travel without paying
das **schwarze** Brett	notice board
das **Schwein** (e)	pig
das **Schweinefleisch**	pork
die **Schweiz/Schweizer**	Switzerland/Swiss
schweizerisch	Swiss
schwer	heavy; difficult
die **Schwester** (n)	sister
die **Schwiegermutter** (¨)	mother-in-law
der **Schwiegersohn** (¨e)	son-in-law
die **Schwiegertochter** (¨)	daughter-in-law
der **Schwiegervater** (¨)	father-in-law
schwierig	difficult
das **Schwimmbad** (¨er)	swimming-baths
schwimmen	to swim
schwindlig	dizzy
schwitzen	to sweat
schwül	sultry
der **See** (n)	lake

die **See**	sea
seekrank	seasick
das **Segelboot** (e)	sailing boat
segeln	to sail
sehen	to see
sehenswert	worth seeing
die **Sehenswürdigkeit** (en)	sight (of interest)
sehr	very
Sehr geehrter Herr!	Dear Sir
die **Seide**	silk
die **Seife**	soap
die **Seilbahn** (en)	cable railway
sein	to be
die **Seite** (n)	side; page
die **Sekretärin** (nen)	secretary
die **Sekunde** (n)	second
selbst	self
selbständig	independent
selbstbewußt	self-confident
die **Selbstbedienung**	self-service (restaurant, etc)
Selbsttanken	self-service (petrol)
selten	seldom
das **Semester** (-)	term
senden	to send
die **Sendung** (en)	programme (TV or radio)
der **Senf**	mustard
der **Sessel** (-)	armchair
sich **setzen**	to sit down
sicher	sure(ly)
der **Sicherheitsgurt** (e)	safety-belt

das **Silber**	silver
singen	to sing
sitzen	to sit
sitzenbleiben	to repeat school year
Ski fahren	to ski
Ski laufen	to ski
die **Socke** (n)	sock
das **Sofa** (s)	sofa
sofort	immediately
sogar	even
der **Sohn** (¨e)	son
der **Soldat** (en)	soldier
sollen	ought
der **Sommer** (-)	summer
der **Sommerschlußverkauf**	summer sales
das **Sonderangebot** (-)	special offer
der **Sonderpreis** (e)	special price
die **Sonne**	sun
sich **sonnen**	to sunbathe
die **Sonnenbrille** (n)	sunglasses
das **Sonnenöl**	suntan lotion
der **Sonnenschein**	sunshine
sonnig	sunny
sonst	otherwise
die **Sorte** (n)	sort
die **Soße** (n)	sauce
die **Sozialkunde**	social studies
Spanien/Spanier	Spain/Spaniard
spanisch	Spanish
spannend	tense
sparen	to save (money)
die **Sparkasse** (n)	bank

der **Spaß**	fun
spät	late
spazierengehen	to go for a walk
der **Spaziergang** (¨-e)	walk
die **Speisekarte** (n)	menu
der **Speisesaal** (... säle)	dining hall
der **Speisewagen** (-)	dining car
die **Sperre** (n)	barrier
die **Spezialität** (en)	speciality
der **Spiegel** (-)	mirror
das **Spiegelei** (er)	fried egg
das **Spiel** (e)	game; match
spielen	to play
das **Spielzeug** (e)	toy
die **Spinne** (n)	spider
Spitze!	Great!
der **Sport**	sport
der **Sportplatz** (¨-e)	sports ground
die **Sprache** (n)	language
das **Sprachlabor** (e)	language laboratory
sprechen	to speak
die **Sprechstunde** (n)	surgery hours
springen	to jump
die **Spritze** (n)	injection
der **Sprudel**	mineral water
spülen	to wash up
die **Spülmaschine** (n)	dishwasher
das **Spülmittel**	washing-up liquid
der **Staat** (en)	state
die **Staatsangehörigkeit**	nationality
das **Stadion** (Stadien)	stadium
die **Stadt** (¨-e)	town

die **Stadtmitte** (n)	town centre
der **Stadtplan** (¨e)	street map
der **Stadtrand** (¨e)	outskirts
das **Stadtteil** (e)	part of town
das **Stadtzentrum** (-zentren)	town centre
der **Stahl**	steel
stark	strong
starten	to start (engine)
der **Staubsauger** (-)	vacuum-cleaner
die **Steckdose** (n)	electric point
stecken	to put
der **Stecker** (-)	plug
stehen	to stand
die **Stehlampe** (n)	standard lamp
stehlen	to steal
steil	steep
der **Stein** (e)	stone
die **Stelle** (n)	place; job
stellen	to put
sterben	to die
die **Stereoanlage** (n)	stereo equipment
der **Stern** (e)	star
der **Stiefel** (-)	boot
still	quiet
stimmen	to be correct
der **Stock** (¨e)	stick; storey
der **Stoff** (e)	material
die **Strafe** (n)	punishment
der **Strand** (e)	beach
die **Straße** (n)	street
die **Straßenbahn** (en)	tram
streichen	to spread

das **Streichholz** (¨-er)	match (for lighting)
der **Streik** (s)	strike
streng	strict
stricken	to knit
der **Strohhalm** (e)	straw (for drinking)
der **Strom** (¨-e)	river
der **Strumpf** (¨-e)	stocking
die **Strumpfhose** (n)	tights
das **Stück** (e)	piece
der **Student** (en)	student
studieren	to study
der **Stuhl** (¨-e)	chair
stumm	dumb
die **Stunde** (n)	hour
der **Stundenplan** (¨-e)	timetable (school)
der **Sturm** (¨-e)	storm
stürmisch	stormy
stürzen	to rush; to fall
suchen	to look for
der **Süden**	south
Super	four-star petrol
der **Supermarkt** (¨-e)	supermarket
die **Suppe** (n)	soup
süß	sweet
die **Süßwaren**	sweets
der **Sylvester**	New Year's Eve
sympathisch	likeable

das **T-shirt**	T-shirt
der **Tabak**	tobacco
das **Tablett** (e)	tray
die **Tablette** (n)	tablet
die **Tafel** (n)	blackboard
die **Tafel** Schokolade	bar of chocolate
der **Tag** (e)	day
die **Tageskarte** (n)	daily menu
die **Tagesschau**	TV news
täglich	daily
das **Tal** (¨er)	valley
die **Talsperre** (n)	dam
tanken	to refuel
die **Tankstelle** (n)	petrol station
die **Tante** (n)	aunt
tanzen	to dance
die **Tapete** (n)	wallpaper
tapezieren	to wallpaper
die **Tasche** (n)	pocket; bag
das **Taschenbuch** (¨er)	paperback book
der **Taschendieb** (e)	pickpocket
das **Taschengeld**	pocket-money
das **Taschentuch** (¨er)	handkerchief
die **Tasse** (n)	cup
taub	deaf
tauchen	to dive
das **Taxi** (s)	taxi
der **Tee**	tea
die **Teekanne** (n)	teapot
teilen	to share
teilnehmen* an	to take part in
der **Teilnehmer** (-)	participant

das **Telefon**	telephone
telefonieren	to telephone
die **Telefonzelle** (n)	telephone box
das **Telegramm** (e)	telegram
der **Teller** (-)	plate
der **Tennisschläger** (-)	tennis racquet
der **Teppich** (e)	carpet
das **Termin** (e)	date (for meeting)
die **Terrasse** (n)	terrace
teuer	expensive
das **Theater** (-)	theatre
die **Theke** (n)	counter
das **Thermometer** (-)	thermometer
tief	deep
das **Tier** (e)	animal
der **Tierarzt** (¨e)	vet
der **Tiger** (-)	tiger
der **Tisch** (e)	table
das **Tischtennis**	table tennis
die **Tochter** (¨)	daughter
der **Tod** (e)	death
die **Toilette** (n)	toilet
Toll!	Great!
die **Tomate** (n)	tomato
das **Tonbandgerät** (e)	tape recorder
der **Topf** (¨e)	pot
das **Tor** (e)	gate; goal (football, etc)
die **Torte** (n)	flan
tot	dead
tragbar	portable
tragen	to carry; to wear

der Topf, Kopf, Knopf.

trainieren	to train
der **Trainingsanzug** (¨-e)	track suit
trampen	to hitch-hike
die **Traube** (n)	grape
träumen	to dream
traurig	sad
treffen	to meet; to hit
der **Treffpunkt** (e)	meeting-place
die **Treppe** (n)	stairs
das **Treppenhaus** (¨-er)	staircase
sich **trimmen**	to keep in trim
trinken	to drink
das **Trinkgeld** (er)	tip
trocken	dry
trocknen	to dry
die **Trompete** (n)	trumpet
der **Tropfen** (-)	drop
trüb	dull
tschüß	'bye
das **Tuch** (¨-er)	cloth
tun	to do
der **Turm** (¨-e)	tower
turnen	to do gymnastics
die **Turnhalle** (n)	gymnasium
die **Tür** (en)	door
die **Tüte** (n)	bag
typisch	typical

die **U-Bahn**	underground railway
die **U-Bahnstation** (en)	underground station
übel	ill
üben	to practise
überall	everywhere
überfahren	to run over
die **Überfahrt** (en)	crossing (by boat, etc)
überfallen	to attack
sich **übergeben**	to be sick
überholen	to overtake
übermorgen	day after tomorrow
übernachten	to stay overnight
überqueren	to cross
überraschen	to surprise
die **Überraschung** (en)	surprise
übersetzen	to translate
die **Übung** (en)	exercise
das **Ufer** (-)	bank (of river)
die **Uhr** (en)	clock
der **Umkleideraum** (¨-e)	changing-room
umkommen*	to die
die **Umleitung** (en)	diversion
ums Leben kommen	to die
der **Umschlag** (¨-e)	envelope
umsonst	in vain; free of charge
umsteigen*	to change (trains, etc)
der **Umtausch** (e)	exchange
umtauschen*	to exchange

umziehen*	to move house
sich **umziehen***	to get changed
unangenehm	unpleasant
unentschieden	undecided
der **Unfall** (¨e)	accident
unfreundlich	unfriendly
ungefähr	approximately
ungenügend	insufficient
ungewöhnlich	unusual
die **Universität** (en)	university
unmöglich	impossible
unrecht haben	to be wrong
unten	downstairs
das **Untergeschoß**	ground floor
die **Unterhaltung** (en)	conversation; entertainment
die **Unterkunft** (¨e)	accommodation
die **Unterrichtsstunde** (n)	lesson
untersagt	forbidden
der **Unterschied** (e)	difference
unterschreiben	to sign
die **Unterschrift** (en)	signature
untersuchen	to examine
die **Untertasse** (n)	saucer
die **Unterwäsche**	underwear
unwahrscheinlich	improbable
der **Urlaub** (e)	holiday
usw	etc

der **Vater** (¨)	father
Vati	Dad
die **Verabredung** (en)	appointment
sich **verabschieden**	to say goodbye
der **Verband** (¨e)	bandage
verbessern	to improve
verbinden	to connect
die **Verbindung** (en)	connection
verboten	forbidden
verbringen	to spend (time)
verdienen	to earn; to deserve
der **Verein** (e)	club
die **Vereinigten** Staaten	United States
sich **verfahren**	to lose your way (by car)
vergessen	to forget
verheiratet	married
sich **verirren**	to get lost
verkaufen	to sell
der **Verkäufer** (-)	salesperson
der **Verkehr**	traffic
das **Verkehrsamt** (¨er)	information office
die **Verkehrsstauung** (en)	traffic jam
verlassen	to leave
sich **verlaufen**	to get lost (on foot)
verletzt	injured
verlieren	to lose
verlobt	engaged
der/die **Verlobte** (n)	fiancé/fiancée
verpassen	to miss (bus, etc)
verreisen	to go away (on holiday)

verschwinden	to disappear
versetzen	to transfer
versichern	to assure
die **Verspätung**	lateness
verstehen	to understand
die **Verstopfung**	constipation
versuchen	to try
vertragen	to bear (i.e. endure)
verunglücken	to have an accident
der/die **Verwandte** (n)	relative
verwundet	wounded
verzeihen	to excuse
Verzeihung!	Excuse me!
verzollen	to declare (at customs)
der **Vetter** (-)	cousin
das **Videogerät** (e)	video recorder
das **Vieh**	cattle
viel	much
Viel Glück!	Good luck!
Viel Spaß!	Have fun!
Viel Vergnügen!	Enjoy yourself!
viele	many
vielen Dank	many thanks
vielleicht	perhaps
das **Viertel** (-)	quarter
der **Vogel** (¨)	bird
voll	full
der **Volleyball**	volleyball
Vollpension	full board
volltanken*	to fill the tank
vorbereiten*	to prepare

die **Vorfahrt**	right of way
vorgestern	day before yesterday
vorhaben*	to intend
der **Vorhang** (¨-e)	curtain
vorher	before
vorig	previous
der **Vormittag** (e)	morning
der **Vorname** (n)	Christian name
vorne	at the front
der **Vorort** (e)	suburb
vorschlagen*	to suggest
die **Vorsicht**	caution
vorsichtig	careful
die **Vorspeise** (n)	hors d'œuvre
(sich) **vorstellen***	to introduce (one-self)
die **Vorstellung** (en)	performance
die **Vorwahlnummer** (n)	dialling code
vorzeigen*	to show
vorziehen*	to prefer

wach	awake
wachsen	to grow
die **Waffe** (n)	weapon
der **Wagen** (-)	car
die **Wahl** (en)	choice
wählen	to choose; to dial
das **Wahlfach** (¨er)	option subject
wahrscheinlich	probable
der **Wald** (¨er)	wood; forest
Wales/Waliser	Wales/Welshman
walisisch	Welsh
die **Wand** (¨e)	wall
wandern	to hike
die **Wanderung** (en)	hike
das **Warenhaus** (¨er)	department store
warm	warm
die **Warnung** (en)	warning
warten	to wait
der **Wartesaal** (.. säle)	waiting-hall
das **Wartezimmer** (-)	waiting-room
warum	why
was fehlt?	what's missing?
was für ...?	what sort of ...?
was ist los?	what's up?
was läuft?	what's on?
das **Waschbecken** (-)	washbasin
die **Wäsche**	washing
waschen	to wash
die **Wäscherei** (en)	laundry
die **Waschmaschine** (n)	washing-machine
das **Waschpulver**	washing-powder
der **Waschraum** (¨e)	washroom

das Pflichtfach

das **Wasser**	water
der **Wasserball**	water polo
der **Wasserhahn** (¨e)	tap
der **Wechsel** (-)	change
wechseln	to change
die **Wechselstube** (n)	currency exchange office
wecken	to wake
der **Wecker** (-)	alarm clock
der **Weg** (e)	path
weg	away
der **Wegweiser** (-)	signpost
wehtun*	to hurt
weiblich	feminine
Weihnachten	Christmas
die **Weile** (n)	while
der **Wein** (e)	wine
weinen	to cry
die **Weinliste** (n)	wine list
die **Weintraube** (n)	bunch of grapes
weiß	white
der **Weißwein**	white wine
weit	far
welch-	which
der **Wellensittich** (e)	budgerigar
die **Welt** (en)	world
die **Weltmeisterschaft** (en)	world championships
wenig	few
werden	to become
werfen	to throw
die **Werkstatt** (¨e)	workshop

der **Werktag** (e)	weekday
die **Wespe** (n)	wasp
der **Westen**	west
das **Wetter**	weather
der **Wetterbericht** (e)	weather report
die **Wettervorhersage** (n)	weather forecast
wichtig	important
wie	how
wieso	why?
wie bitte?	pardon?
wie geht's?	how are you?
wie schade!	what a pity!
wieder	again
wiederholen	to repeat
wiegen	to weigh
Wien	Vienna
die **Wiese** (n)	meadow
wieviel (e)	how much (many)
Willkommen	welcome
der **Wind**	wind
windig	windy
die **Windschutzscheibe** (n)	windscreen
wirklich	really
die **Wirtschaft** (en)	public house; economy
das **Wirtshaus** (¨er)	public house
wissen	to know
die **Witwe** (n)	widow
die **Woche** (n)	week
das **Wochenende** (n)	weekend
wöchentlich	weekly
woher?	where from?

sich **wohlfühlen***	to feel well
wohnen	to live
der **Wohnort** (e)	residence
die **Wohnung** (en)	flat
der **Wohnwagen** (-)	caravan
das **Wohnzimmer** (-)	living room
die **Wolke** (n)	cloud
wolkenlos	cloudless
wolkig	cloudy
wollen	to want
die **Wolle**	wool
das **Wort** (¨er/e)	word
das **Wörterbuch** (¨er)	dictionary
die **Wunde** (n)	wound
wunderbar	wonderful
der **Wunsch** (¨e)	wish
wünschen	to wish
die **Wurst** (¨e)	sausage

ABCDEFGHIJKLMNOPQRSTUVWXY**Z**

zahlen	to pay
zählen	to count
der **Zahn** (¨e)	tooth
der **Zahnarzt** (¨e)	dentist

die **Zahnbürste** (n)	toothbrush
die **Zahnpasta**	toothpaste
z.B.	e.g.
zeichnen	to draw
zeigen	to show
die **Zeit** (en)	time
die **Zeitschrift** (en)	magazine
die **Zeitung** (en)	newspaper
das **Zelt** (e)	tent
zelten	to camp
die **Zentralheizung**	central heating
das **Zentrum** (Zentren)	centre
zerstören	to destroy
der **Zettel** (–)	note; piece of paper
der **Zeuge** (n)	witness
das **Zeugnis** (se)	school report
ziehen	to pull
das **Ziel** (e)	target
ziemlich	quite
die **Zigarette** (n)	cigarette
die **Zigarre** (n)	cigar
das **Zimmer** (–)	room
die **Zitrone** (n)	lemon
der **Zoll**	customs
der **Zollbeamte** (n)	customs officer
zollfrei	duty-free
die **Zollkontrolle** (n)	customs inspection
der **Zoo**	zoo
zu Fuß	on foot
zu Mittag essen	to have lunch
der **Zucker**	sugar
zuerst	at first

zufrieden	satisfied
der **Zug** (¨e)	train
zuhören*	to listen
zum Mitnehmen	take-away
zum Wohl!	Cheers!
zumachen*	to close
die **Zunge** (n)	tongue
zurückkommen*	to return
zusammen	together
der **Zusammenstoß** (¨e)	collision
der **Zuschauer** (-)	spectator
der **Zuschlag** (¨e)	extra payment
der **Zwilling** (e)	twin
die **Zwiebel** (n)	onion

ENGLISH—GERMAN

Bitte, nehmen Sie dieses Geschenk an.

present < anwesend / das Geschenk

abroad	das Ausland
absent	abwesend
to **accelerate**	Gas geben
to **accept**	annehmen*
Access Only	Anlieger frei
accident	der Unfall
accommodation	die Unterkunft
to **accompany**	begleiten
achievement	die Leistung
acquaintance	der/die Bekannte
action	die Handlung
actor	der Schauspieler
address	die Adresse; die Anschrift
to **admire**	bewundern
admission ticket	die Eintrittskarte
adult	der/die Erwachsene
adventure	das Abenteuer
advertisement	die Reklame
to **advise**	raten
aeroplane	das Flugzeug
afternoon	der Nachmittag
afterwards	nachher
again	wieder
age	das Alter
agreed	einverstanden
air	die Luft
air-bed	die Luftmatraze
airmail	die Luftpost
airport	der Flughafen
A-levels	das Abitur
alarm clock	der Wecker

alcohol	der Alkohol
all	all-
all the best	alles Gute
to **allow**	erlauben
allowed	gestattet
almost	fast
alone	allein
already	schon
also	auch
always	immer
ambulance	der Krankenwagen
America	Amerika
American	Amerikaner/ amerikanisch
angry	böse
animal	das Tier
announcer	der Ansager
annual	jährlich
anorak	der Anorak
answer	die Antwort
to **answer**	antworten; beantworten
to **apologize**	sich entschuldigen
apparatus	der Apparat
to **appear**	erscheinen
apple	der Apfel
apple juice	der Apfelsaft
appointment	der Verabredung
apprentice	der Lehrling
apprenticeship	die Lehre
approximately	ungefähr
area	die Gegend

arm	der Arm
armchair	der Sessel
to **arrange** in order	einordnen*
arrival	die Ankunft *
to **arrive**	ankommen*
art	die Kunst
article	der Artikel
artist	der Künstler
ashtray	der Aschenbecher
to **ask**	fragen
to **ask** a question	eine Frage stellen
to **ask** for	bitten um
to **assure**	versichern
at first	zuerst
at last	endlich
at once	sofort; gleich
at that time	damals
at the back	hinten
at the front	vorne
athletics	die Athletik; die Leichtathletik
to **attack**	überfallen
Attention!	Achtung!
attic	der Dachboden
aunt	die Tante
Austria/ Austrian	Österreich/ Osterreicher/ österreichisch
available	erhältlich
awake	wach
away	weg

* die Auskunft = information

baby	das Baby
back	der Rücken
bad	schlecht; schlimm
bad luck	das Pech
badminton	der Federball
bag	die Tasche; die Tüte
bake	backen
baker	der Bäcker
baker's shop	die Bäckerei
balcony	der Balkon
bald head	die Glatze
ball	der Ball
ballpoint pen	der Kugelschreiber (Kuli)
Baltic Sea	die Ostsee
banana	die Banane
band	die Kapelle; die Band
bandage	der Verband
bank	die Bank; die Sparkasse
bank (of river)	das Ufer
to **barbecue**	grillen
bar of chocolate	die Tafel Schokolade
barrier	die Sperre
basket	der Korb
bat (e.g. cricket)	der Schläger
bath	das Bad
bath towel	das Badetuch
bath-tub	die Badewanne
bathe	baden
bathing costume	der Badeanzug
bathroom	das Badezimmer

battery — die Batterie
to **be** — sein
to **be** able — können
to **be** allowed — dürfen
to **be** bored — sich langweilen
to **be** called (i.e. named) — heißen
to **be** correct — stimmen
to **be** enough — genügen
to **be** in detention — nachsitzen*
to **be** interested — sich interessieren für
to **be** missing — fehlen
to **be** pleased — sich freuen
to **be** right — recht haben
to **be** sick (i.e. vomit) — sich übergeben
to **be** situated — sich befinden
to **be** wrong — unrecht haben
beach — der Strand
bean — die Bohne
to **bear** (i.e. endure) — leiden; vertragen
beard — der Bart
beautiful — schön
to **become** — werden
bed — das Bett
bedclothes — die Bettwäsche
bedroom — das Schlafzimmer
bedside table — der Nachttisch
bee — die Biene
beef — das Rindfleisch
beer — das Bier
before — vorher
to **begin** — beginnen

to **behave**	sich benehmen
Belgium	Belgien
Belgian	Belgier/belgisch
to **believe**	glauben
belly	der Bauch
to **belong**	gehören
belt	der Gürtel
bench	die Bank
better	besser
bicycle	das Fahrrad
big	groß
bill	die Rechnung
biology	die Biologie
bird	der Vogel
birth	die Geburt
birthday	der Geburtstag
biscuit	der Keks
to **bite**	beißen
black	schwarz
blackboard	die Tafel
blanket	die Bettdecke
to **bleed**	bluten
Bless you! (on sneezing)	Gesundheit!
blind	blind
blocked	gesperrt
blond	blond
blood	das Blut
blouse	die Bluse
blue	blau
board	das Brett
boarding-house	die Pension
boat	das Boot

body	der Körper
book	das Buch
to **book**	buchen
boot	der Stiefel
boot (of car)	der Kofferraum
border	die Grenze
boring	langweilig
born	geboren
to **borrow**	borgen
boss	der Chef
both	beide
bottle	die Flasche
bottle-opener	der Flaschenöffner
bowl	die Schale
bowl of ice-cream	der Eisbecher
boy	der Junge
boy scout	der Pfadfinder
box	die Schachtel
bra	der Büstenhalter
brake	die Bremse
to **brake**	bremsen
brand	die Marke
brass band	die Blaskapelle
bread	das Brot
bread and butter	das Butterbrot
bread roll	das Brötchen
to **break**	brechen
break-time (at school)	die Pause
breakdown (mechanical)	die Panne
breakfast	das Frühstück
to **breakfast**	frühstücken
breathless	atemlos

bridge	die Brücke
briefcase	die Mappe
bright	hell
to **bring**	bringen
broadcasting	der Rundfunk
brochure	die Broschüre
broken	kaputt
brother	der Bruder
brother-in-law	der Schwager
brothers and sisters	die Geschwister
brown	braun
brush	die Bürste
to **brush**	bürsten
budgerigar	der Wellensittich
to **build**	bauen
building	das Gebäude
building site	die Baustelle
bunch of grapes	die Weintraube
burglar	der Einbrecher
to **burn**	brennen
burst tyre	die Reifenpanne
bus	der Bus
business hours	die Geschäftszeiten
businessman	der Geschäftsmann
busy	beschäftigt
butcher	der Metzger
butcher's shop	die Metzgerei
butter	die Butter
button	der Knopf
to **buy**	kaufen
to **buy** (tickets)	lösen
'bye	tschüß

cabbage	der Kohl
cable railway	die Seilbahn
café	das Café
cage	der Käfig
cake	der Kuchen
to **calculate**	rechnen
calculator	der Rechner
to **call**	rufen
to **call** (i.e. name)	nennen
to **call up** (telephone)	anrufen*
calm	die Ruhe
calm	ruhig
camera	der Fotoapparat
to **camp**	zelten
camp-site	der Campingplatz
can (to be able)	können
canal	der Kanal
candle	die Kerze
cap	die Mütze
car	das Auto; der Wagen; der PKW
caravan	der Wohnwagen
card	die Karte
careful	vorsichtig
caretaker	der Hausmeister
carnival	der Fasching
car park	der Parkplatz
carpet	der Teppich
carrot	die Möhre
to **carry**	tragen
case (instance)	der Fall
cashdesk	die Kasse

cashier	der Kassierer
cassette	die Kassette
cassette recorder	der Kassettenrekord-er
castle	die Burg; das Schloß
cat	die Katze
to **catch**	fangen
cathedral	der Dom
cattle	das Vieh
cauliflower	der Blumenkohl
caution	die Vorsicht
ceiling	die Decke
cellar	der Keller
cemetery	der Friedhof
central heating	die Zentralheizung
centre	das Zentrum
century	das Jahrhundert
certain(ly)	bestimmt; gewiß
chain	die Kette
chair	der Stuhl
chalk	die Kreide
change	der Wechsel
to **change**	wechseln
change (i.e. money)	das Kleingeld
to **change** (cheques)	einlösen*
to **change** (trains, etc)	umsteigen*
changing-room	der Umkleideraum
channel	der Kanal
chapel	die Kapelle
to **chat**	plaudern
cheap	billig; preiswert
to **cheat**	mogeln

to **check**	kontrollieren
checked	kariert
cheeky	frech
Cheers!	Prost!
cheese	der Käse
chemist's (dispensing)	die Apotheke
chemist's	die Drogerie
chemistry	die Chemie
cheque	der Scheck
cheque card	die Scheckkarte
cherry	die Kirsche
chess	das Schach
chest	die Brust
to **chew**	kauen
chewing-gum	der Kaugummi
chicken (roast, etc)	das Hähnchen
chicken	das Huhn
child	das Kind
chips	die Pommes Frites
chocolate (in a box)	die Praline
chocolate	die Schokolade
choice	die Wahl
to **choose**	wählen
Christian name	der Vorname
Christmas	Weihnachten
Christmas Eve	der Heilige Abend
church	die Kirche
church service	der Gottesdienst
cigar	die Zigarre
cigarette	die Zigarrette
cigarette lighter	das Feuerzeug
cinema	das Kino

circle	der Kreis
circular tour	die Rundfahrt
city	die Großstadt
class	die Klasse
class test	die Klassenarbeit
class trip	die Klassenfahrt
classical	klassisch
classmate	der Klassenkamerad
classroom	das Klassenzimmer
clean	sauber
to **clean**	sauber machen; putzen
clear	klar
to **clear** away	abräumen*
clever	klug
climate	das Klima
to **climb**	klettern
clinic	die Klinik
cloakroom	die Garderobe
clock	die Uhr
to **close**	schließen; zumachen*
closed	geschlossen
closing-day	der Ruhetag
closing-time	der Feierabend
cloth	das Tuch; der Lappen
clothes	die Kleider
clothing	die Kleidung
cloud	die Wolke
cloudless	wolkenlos
cloudy	wolkig; bewölkt

club	der Verein
coach	der Reisebus
coal	die Kohle
coast	die Küste
coat	der Mantel
Coca-Cola	die Cola
cocoa	der Kakao
coffee	der Kaffee
coffee-pot	die Kaffeekanne
coin	die Münze
cold	kalt
cold (illness)	die Erkältung; der Schnupfen
cold (-ness)	die Kälte
cold buffet	die kalte Platte
cold meat slices	der Aufschnitt
to **collect**	sammeln
collection	die Sammlung
college	die Hochschule
collision	der Zusammenstoß
Cologne	Köln
colour	die Farbe
colourful	bunt
comb	der Kamm
to **comb**	kämmen
to **come**	kommen
comedy	die Komödie
comfortable	bequem
common	allgemein
compartment	das Abteil
to **complain**	sich beschweren; beklagen

complicated	kompliziert
comprehensive school	die Gesamtschule
compulsory subject	das Pflichtfach
computer	der Computer
computer studies	die Informatik
concert	das Konzert
conduct (behaviour)	die Führung
conductor (trains, etc)	der Schaffner
confectioner's shop	die Konditorei
to **congratulate**	gratulieren
congratulations	herzlichen Glückwunsch
to **connect**	verbinden
connection	die Verbindung
constipation	die Verstopfung
conversation	das Gespräch; die Unterhaltung
cook	der Koch
to **cook**	kochen
cooker	der Herd
cool	kühl
to **copy**	abschreiben*
corner	die Ecke
correct	richtig
corridor	der Gang
to **cost**	kosten
costly	kostbar
costume	das Kostüm
cosy	gemütlich
cotton	die Baumwolle
couchette	der Liegewagen
to **cough**	husten

to **count**	zählen
counter	der Schalter; die Theke
country	das Land
countryside	die Landschaft
court	der Hof
cousin (*f*)	die Kusine
cousin (*m*)	der Vetter
to **cover**	decken
cow	die Kuh
cream	die Sahne
crisps	die Chips
crockery	das Geschirr
to **cross**	überqueren
cross ...	Quer ...
crossing (by boat, etc)	die Überfahrt
crossroads	die Kreuzung
crowd	die Menge
to **cry**	weinen
cuckoo clock	die Kuckucksuhr
cucumber	die Gurke
cup	die Tasse
cup (trophy)	der Pokal
cupboard	der Schrank
cure	die Kur
curious	neugierig
current	aktuell
curtain	der Vorhang
cushion	das Kissen
customer	der Kunde
customs	der Zoll
customs inspection	die Zollkontrolle

customs officer	der Zollbeamte
to **cut**	schneiden
cutlery	das Besteck
cutlet	das Kotelett; das Schnitzel
to **cycle**	radfahren*
cyclist	der Radfahrer

ABCDEFGHIJKLMNOPQRSTUVWXYZ

Dad	Vati
daily	täglich
daily menu	die Tageskarte
dam	die Talsperre
damp	feucht
to **dance**	tanzen
danger	die Gefahr
danger to life	die Lebensgefahr
dangerous	gefährlich
Danube	die Donau
dark	dunkel
date	das Datum
date (for meeting)	das Termin
date of birth	das Geburtsdatum
daughter	die Tochter

daughter-in-law	die Schwieger-tochter
day	der Tag
day after tomorrow	übermorgen
day before yesterday	vorgestern
dead	tot
deaf	taub
Dear Sir	Sehr geehrter Herr!
death	der Tod
to **decide**	beschließen; sich entschließen
to **declare** (at customs)	verzollen
deep	tief
deficient	mangelhaft
degree	der Grad
delicious	lecker
to **deliver**	liefern
delivery van	der Lieferwagen
dentist	der Zahnarzt
to **depart**	abfahren*
department	die Abteilung
department store	das Kaufhaus; das Warenhaus
departure	die Abfahrt
to **depend** on	abhängen* von
to **describe**	beschreiben
description	die Beschreibung
to **deserve**	verdienen
desk	das Pult
to **destroy**	zerstören
detached house	das Einfamilien-haus

to **dial**	wählen
dialling code	die Vorwahl
diarrhoea	der Durchfall
dictionary	das Wörterbuch
to **die**	sterben; umkommen*; ums Leben kommen
difference	der Unterschied
different	anders
difficult	schwer; schwierig
dining car	der Speisewagen
dining hall	der Speisesaal
dining room	das Eßzimmer
direct	direkt
direction	die Richtung
dirty	schmutzig; dreckig
disabled	körperbehindert
to **disappear**	verschwinden
discotheque	die Diskothek
to **discover**	entdecken
dish	die Schüssel
dishwasher	die Spülmaschine
distance	die Entfernung
to **dive**	tauchen
diversion	die Umleitung
dizzy	schwindlig
to **do**	machen; tun
to **do** gymnastics	turnen
to **do** the shopping	Einkäufe machen
doctor	der Arzt
dog	der Hund
doll	die Puppe

don't mention it	nichts zu danken
door	die Tür
double room	das Doppelzimmer
downstairs	unten
dozen	das Dutzend
to **draw**	zeichnen
to **dream**	träumen
dress	das Kleid
drink	das Getränk
to **drink**	trinken
to **drive**	fahren
driver	der Fahrer
driving licence	der Führerschein
to **drop**	fallenlassen
drop (of water)	der Tropfen
drunk	betrunken
dry	trocken
to **dry**	trocknen
duck	die Ente
dull	trüb
dumb	stumm
dumpling	der Knödel
Dutch	holländisch
Dutchman	Holländer
duty	die Pflicht
duty-free	zollfrei
duvet	das Federbett

e.g.	z.B.
ear	das Ohr
early	früh
to **earn**	verdienen
earth	die Erde
east	der Osten
Easter	Ostern
East Germany	die DDR
to **eat**	essen
to **eat** (of animals)	fressen
economy	die Wirtschaft
E(E)C	die E(W)G
egg	das Ei
electric	elektrisch
electric cooker	der Elektroherd
electric point	die Steckdose
electrician	der Elektriker
elephant	der Elefant
emergency exit	der Notausgang
emergency service	der Notdienst
employee	der/die Angestellte; der Arbeitnehmer
employer	der Arbeitgeber
empty	leer
to **empty**	leermachen*
to **enclose**	beilegen*
end	das Ende
to **end**	beenden
engaged	verlobt
engine	der Motor
engineer	der Ingenieur
England/Englishman	England/Engländer

English	englisch
Enjoy yourself!	Viel Vergnügen!
enough	genug
to **enter**	betreten
entertainment	die Unterhaltung
entrance (e.g. car park)	die Einfahrt
entrance (e.g. shop)	der Eingang
entrance (e.g. bus)	der Einstieg
envelope	der Umschlag
escalator	die Rolltreppe
especially	besonders
essay	der Aufsatz
etc	usw
Europe	Europa
European	Europäer/ europäisch
even	sogar
evening	der Abend
evening meal	das Abendessen
every	jed-
everything	alles
everywhere	überall
exact(ly)	genau
to **examine**	untersuchen
examination	die Prüfung
example	das Beispiel
excellent	ausgezeichnet
exchange	der Austausch; der Umtausch
to **exchange**	umtauschen*
exchange rate	der Kurs
excursion	der Ausflug

to **excuse**	entschuldigen; verzeihen
Excuse me!	Entschuldigung! Verzeihung!
exercise	die Übung
exercise book	das Heft
exertion	die Anstrengung
exhibition	die Ausstellung
exit (e.g. car park)	die Ausfahrt
exit (e.g. shop)	der Ausgang
exit (e.g. bus)	der Ausstieg
expensive	teuer
experience	die Erfahrung
to **explain**	erklären
explanation	die Erklärung
express cleaners	die Schnellreinigung
express train	der Eilzug; der Schnellzug
expression	der Ausdruck
extra payment	der Zuschlag
eye	das Auge

ABCDEFGHIJKLMNOPQRSTUVWXYZ

face	das Gesicht
factory	die Fabrik
to **fail**	durchfallen*

fall	der Fall
to **fall**	fallen; stürzen
to **fall** asleep	einschlafen*
family	die Familie
famous	berühmt
far	weit
fare	der Fahrpreis
farm	der Bauernhof
farmer	der Bauer
fashion	die Mode
fast	schnell
fat	dick
father	der Vater
father-in-law	der Schwiegervater
favourable	günstig
favourite	der Liebling
favourite subject	das Lieblingsfach
fear	die Angst
fee	die Gebühr
to **feed**	füttern
to **feel**	fühlen
to **feel** well	sich wohlfühlen*
felt-tip pen	der Filzstift
feminine	weiblich
ferry	die Fähre
to **fetch**	holen
few	wenig
fiancé/fiancée	der/die Verlobte
field	das Feld
to **fill**	füllen
to **fill** the tank	volltanken*
film	der Film

final (sport)	das Endspiel
final examination	die Abschlußprüfung
finally	schließlich
to **find**	finden
to **find** out	erfahren
fine (penalty)	die Geldstrafe
finger	der Finger
finish	der Schluß
finished	fertig
fire	das Feuer
fire brigade	die Feuerwehr
fire engine	der Feuerwehrwagen
fire extinguisher	der Feuerlöscher
fireplace	der Kamin
firm	die Firma
first aid	erste Hilfe
fish	der Fisch
to **fish**	angeln
fishing-rod	die Angelrute
to **fit**	passen
flan	die Torte
flat	flach
flat	die Wohnung
flight	der Flug
floor	der Fußboden
to **flow**	fließen
flower	die Blume
fluent	fließend
flute	die Flöte
fly	die Fliege

to **fly**	fliegen
fog	der Nebel
foggy	neblig
to **fold**	klappen
folding chair	der Klappstuhl
folding table	der Klapptisch
to **follow**	folgen
food	das Essen
foot	der Fuß
football	der Fußball
football ground	der Fußballplatz
for a long time	lange
forbidden	untersagt; verboten
foreign language	die Fremdsprache
foreigner	der Ausländer
forest	der Forst; der Wald
to **forget**	vergessen
fork	die Gabel
form (paper)	das Formular
form captain	der Klassensprecher
form teacher	der Klassenlehrer
fountain pen	der Füller
four star petrol	Super
France	Frankreich
free	frei
free of charge	kostenlos; umsonst
freeze	frieren
fresh	frisch
fried egg	das Spiegelei
fried sausage	die Bratwurst
friend	der Freund
friendly	freundlich

fruit	die Frucht; das Obst
full	voll
full (after meal)	satt
full board	Vollpension
fun	der Spaß
to **function**	funktionieren
funny	komisch; lustig
furnished	möbliert
furniture	das Möbel

ABCDEFGHIJKLMNOPQRSTUVWXYZ

game	das Spiel
garage	die Garage
garden	der Garten
gate	das Tor
gender	das Geschlecht
general	allgemein
generous	großzügig
gentleman	der Herr
Gentlemen	Herren
genuine	echt
geography	die Erdkunde; die Geographie

German	Deutscher/deutsch
German Automobile Club	der ADAC
German Railways	die Deutsche Bundesbahn
Germany	Deutschland
to **get**	bekommen; besorgen; kriegen
to **get** annoyed	sich ärgern
to **get** changed	sich umziehen*
to **get** dressed	sich anziehen*
to **get** lost	sich verirren; sich verlaufen
to **get** off	aussteigen*
to **get** on	einsteigen*
to **get** to know	kennenlernen
to **get** undressed	sich ausziehen*
to **get** up	aufstehen*
Get well soon!	Gute Besserung!
girl	das Mädchen
to **give**	geben; schenken
to **give** (details, etc)	angeben*
to **give** up	aufgeben*
glad	froh
glass	das Glas
glove	der Handschuh
to **go**	fahren; gehen
to **go** away (on holiday)	verreisen
to **go** for a walk	spazierengehen
to **go** out	ausgehen*
goal	das Tor
God	der Gott
gold	das Gold

good	gut
Good evening	Guten Abend
Good luck!	viel Glück!
Good morning	Guten Morgen
goodbye	auf Wiedersehen
goodbye (telephone)	auf Wiederhören
Good day	Guten Tag
Good night	Gute Nacht
goose	die Gans
grammar school	das Gymnasium
gram(me)	das Gramm
grandad	der Opa
grandfather	der Großvater
grandma	die Oma
grandmother	die Großmutter
grandparents	die Großeltern
grandson	der Enkel
grape	die Traube
grass	das Gras
grateful	dankbar
great	großartig
Great!	Klasse! Prima! Toll! Spitze!
green	grün
greet	grüßen; begrüßen
greeting	der Gruß
grey	grau
grocer's shop	das Lebensmittelgeschäft
groceries	die Lebensmittel
ground	der Boden

ground floor	das Erdgeschoß; das Parterre; das Untergeschoß
group	die Gruppe
to **grow**	wachsen
to **guess**	raten
guest	der Gast
guide	der Führer; der Reiseleiter
guide-book	der Reiseführer
guinea-pig	das Meerschweinchen
guitar	die Gitarre
gymnasium	die Turnhalle

ABCDEFG**H**IJKLMNOPQRSTUVWXYZ

habit	die Gewohnheit
hail (frozen rain)	der Hagel
to **hail**	hageln
hair	das Haar
hairbrush	die Haarbürste
hairdresser	der Friseur
hair-dryer	der Haartrockner
half	die Hälfte

half	halb
half-board	Halbpension
hall	der Flur; der Saal
ham	der Schinken
hamster	der Hamster
hand	die Hand
to **hand in**	einreichen*
handbag	die Handtasche
handicraft	die Handarbeiten
handkerchief	das Taschentuch
to **happen**	geschehen; passieren
happiness	das Glück
happy	glücklich
harbour	der Hafen
hard	hart
hard-working	fleißig
hardly	kaum
hat	der Hut
to **have**	haben
to **have** a cold	erkältet sein
Have a good journey!	Gute Reise!
to **have** a hangover	einen Kater haben
to **have** a light	Feuer haben
to **have** a rest	sich ausruhen*
to **have** a shower	sich duschen
to **have** a temperature	Fieber haben
to **have** an accident	verunglücken
Have fun!	viel Spaß!
to **have** lunch	zu Mittag essen
to **have** on (i.e. wear)	anhaben*
head	der Kopf

headmaster	der Direktor
headlamp	der Scheinwerfer
health	die Gesundheit
health insurance	die Krankenkasse
health resort	der Kurort
healthy	gesund
hear	hören
heart	das Herz
heat	die Hitze
to **heat**	heizen
heating	die Heizung
heaven	der Himmel
heavy	schwer
helicopter	der Hubschrauber
Hello!	Grüß Gott!
help	die Hilfe
to **help**	helfen
to **help** oneself	sich bedienen
here	hier
high	hoch
high jump	der Hochsprung
hike	die Wanderung
to **hike**	wandern
hill	der Hügel
history	die Geschichte
to **hit**	schlagen; treffen
to **hitch-hike**	per Anhalter fahren; trampen
hobby	das Hobby
to **hold**	halten
to **hold** tight	festhalten*
holiday	der Urlaub

holidays	die Ferien
Holland	Holland
homeland	die Heimat
homesickness	das Heimweh
homework	die Hausaufgabe
honest	ehrlich
honey	der Honig
to **hope**	hoffen
hors d'oeuvre	die Vorspeise
horse	das Pferd
hospital	das Krankenhaus
host	der Gastgeber
hostel warden (*f*)	die Herbergsmutter
hostel warden (*m*)	der Herbergsvater
hot	heiß
hotel	das Hotel
hour	die Stunde
house	das Haus
house number	die Hausnummer
household	der Haushalt
housewife	die Hausfrau
how	wie
how are you?	wie geht's?
how much (many)	wieviel (e)
hunger	der Hunger
to **hurry**	eilen; sich beeilen
to **hurt**	schmerzen; wehtun*
hut	die Hütte

I am sorry	es tut mir leid
I hope	hoffentlich
I would like	ich hätte gern; ich möchte
ice	das Eis
ice-cream	das Eis
idea (notion)	die Ahnung
idea	die Idee
ill	krank; übel
illness	die Krankheit
immediately	sofort
important	wichtig
impossible	unmöglich
improbable	unwahrscheinlich
to **improve**	verbessern
in a bad mood	schlechter Laune
in a good mood	guter Laune
in confusion	durcheinander
in the middle of	inmitten
in the open air	im Freien
in vain	umsonst
in writing	schriftlich
included	inbegriffen
inclusive	inklusive
independent	selbständig
indoor swimming-pool	das Hallenbad
industry	die Industrie
influenza	die Grippe
information	die Auskunft
information office	das Informationsbüro; das Verkehrsamt

inhabitant	der Einwohner
injection	die Spritze
injured	verletzt
to **inquire** about	sich erkundigen nach
insect	das Insekt
instructions for use	die Gebrauchsanweisungen
instrument	das Instrument
insufficient	ungenügend
intelligent	intelligent
to **intend**	vorhaben*
interest	das Interesse
interesting	interessant
to introduce (oneself)	(sich) vorstellen*
invitation	die Einladung
to **invite**	einladen*
Ireland	Irland
Irish/Irishman	irisch/Irländer
to **iron**	bügeln
island	die Insel
Italian	Italiener/italienisch
Italy	Italien
it doesn't matter	es macht nichts
it's all the same to me	es ist mir egal

jacket	die Jacke
jam	die Marmelade
jewellery	der Schmuck
job	die Stelle
journey	die Fahrt; die Reise
juice	der Saft
to **jump**	springen
just	gerade

ABCDEFGHIJ**K**LMNOPQRSTUVWXYZ

to **keep** in trim	sich trimmen
to **keep** free	freihalten *
to **keep** one's distance	Abstand halten
key	der Schlüssel
kilogram(me)	das Kilo
kiosk	der Kiosk
kitchen	die Küche
knee	das Knie
knife	das Messer
to **knit**	stricken
to **knock**	klopfen
to **know**	kennen; wissen

laboratory	das Labor
Ladies	Damen
lady	die Frau
lake	der See
Lake Constance	der Bodensee
lamb	das Lamm
lamp	die Lampe
language	die Sprache
language laboratory	das Sprachlabor
last	letzt-
to **last**	dauern
late	spät
lateness	die Verspätung
Latin	das Latein
to **laugh**	lachen
lawn	der Rasen
lazy	faul
to **lead**	führen
leaf	das Blatt
to **lean out**	hinauslehnen*
to **learn**	lernen
leather	das Leder
to **leave**	verlassen
left	link-
left-luggage office	die Gepäckaufbewahrung
leg	das Bein
leisure time	die Freizeit
lemon	die Zitrone
lemonade	die Limonade
to **lend**	leihen
lesson	die Unterrichtsstunde

to **let**	lassen
letter	der Brief
letter-box	der Briefkasten
lettuce	der Kopfsalat
library	die Bibliothek
to **lie** (on bed, etc)	liegen
to **lie** down	sich hinlegen*
lift (in hotel, etc)	der Aufzug; der Fahrstuhl
light	hell
light	das Licht
lightning	der Blitz
to **like**	gern haben; mögen
likeable	sympathisch
likewise	gleichfalls
line	die Linie
lion	der Löwe
list	die Liste
list of drinks	die Getränkekarte
to **listen**	zuhören*
litter	der Abfall
little	klein
litre	das Liter
to **live**	leben; wohnen
lively	lebhaft
liver sausage	die Leberwurst
living-room	das Wohnzimmer
loaf	das Brot
local call	das Ortsgespräch
local train	der Nahverkehrszug
to **lock** up	abschließen*
locker	das Schließfach

long	lang
look	der Blick
to **look**	gucken; schauen
to **look** (i.e. appear)	aussehen*
to **look** at	ansehen*
to **look** for	suchen
to **look** forward to	sich freuen auf
lorry	der Lastwagen; der LKW
to **lose**	verlieren
to **lose** weight	abnehmen
to **lose** your way (e.g. by car)	sich verfahren
lost-property office	das Fundbüro
loud	laut
love	lieben
LP record	die Langspielplatte
luck	das Glück
luggage	das Gepäck
luggage-rack	das Gepäcknetz
luggage trolley	der Kofferkuli

machine	der Automat; die Maschine
magazine	die Illustrierte; die Zeitschrift
magnificent	herrlich
main station	der Hauptbahnhof
main street	die Hauptstraße
to **make**	machen
to **make** room	Platz machen
man	der Mann
many	viele
many thanks	vielen Dank
map	die Landkarte
margarine	die Margarine
mark (for school work)	die Note
market	der Markt
market-place	der Marktplatz
married	verheiratet
married couple	das Ehepaar
marry	heiraten
masculine	männlich
mashed potato	der Kartoffelbrei
match (for lighting)	das Streichholz
match (i.e. game)	das Spiel
material	der Stoff
maths	die Mathe
mayor	der Bürgermeister
meadow	die Wiese
meal	das Essen
to **mean**	bedeuten
meat	das Fleisch
mechanic	der Mechaniker

medical certificate	der Krankenschein
medicament	das Medikament
medicine	die Medizin
Mediterranean Sea	das Mittelmeer
meet	abholen*; treffen
meeting-place	der Treffpunkt
member	das Mitglied
men's fashion	die Herrenmode
menswear	die Herrenkonfektion
menu	die Speisekarte
merchant	der Kaufmann
merry	fröhlich
midday	der Mittag
midday meal	das Mittagessen
middle	die Mitte
midge	die Mücke
midnight	die Mitternacht
mild	mild
mile	die Meile
milk	die Milch
mineral water	das Mineralwasser; der Sprudel
minute	die Minute
mirror	der Spiegel
to **miss** (e.g. miss the bus)	verpassen
Miss	Fräulein
mistake	der Fehler
misunderstanding	das Mißverständnis
mixed	gemischt
modern	modern
moment	das Moment; der Augenblick

money	das Geld
monkey	der Affe
month	der Monat
monthly	monatlich
monument	das Denkmal
moon	der Mond
moped	das Mofa
more	mehr
morning	der Morgen; der Vormittag
mother	die Mutter
mother-in-law	die Schwiegermutter
motorbike	das Motorrad
motorway	die Autobahn
mountain	der Berg
mountains	das Gebirge
mouse	die Maus
moustache	der Schnurrbart
mouth	der Mund
to **move**	sich bewegen
to **move** house	umziehen*
to **mow**	mähen
Mr	Herr
Mrs	Frau
much	viel
multi-storey car park	das Parkhaus
Mum	Mutti
Munich	München
museum	das Museum
mushroom	der Pilz; der Champignon
music	die Musik

musician	der Musiker
must	müssen
mustard	der Senf

ABCDEFGHIJKLMNOPQRSTUVWXYZ

nail	der Nagel
name	der Name
name-day	der Namenstag
narrow	eng; schmal
nationality	die Staatsangehörigkeit
natural(ly)	natürlich
nature	die Natur
near	in der Nähe von
to **need**	brauchen
neighbour	der Nachbar
nephew	der Neffe
nervous	nervös
net	das Netz
the **Netherlands**	die Niederlande
never	nie
new	neu
New Year	das Neujahr
New Year's Eve	Sylvester

news	die Nachrichten
newspaper	die Zeitung
next	nächst-
next-door	nebenan
nice	nett
niece	die Nichte
night	die Nacht
no	nein
no longer	nicht mehr
No Parking	Parkverbot
nobody	niemand
noise	der Lärm
non-smoker	der Nichtraucher
nonsense	der Blödsinn; der Quatsch
north	der Norden
North Sea	die Nordsee
not	nicht
not at all	gar nicht
not until	erst um
not yet	noch nicht
note (banknote)	der Schein
note (piece of paper)	der Zettel
notebook	das Notizbuch
nothing	nichts
notice board	das schwarze Brett
nought	null
novel	der Roman
now	jetzt; nun
number	die Nummer
nurse	die Krankenschwester

obvious(ly)	offensichtlich
occupied	besetzt
to **offer**	bieten; anbieten *
office	das Büro
office hours	die Geschäftszeiten
official	der Beamte
often	oft
oil	das Öl
old	alt
omelette	das Omelett
on board	an Bord
on foot	zu Fuß
once	einmal
once again	noch einmal
one	man
one and a half	anderthalb
one-way street	die Einbahnstraße
onion	die Zwiebel
only	nur
only child	das Einzelkind
open	geöffnet; offen
to **open**	aufmachen *; öffnen
open-air swimming baths	das Freibad
opening hours	die Öffnungszeiten
opinion	die Meinung
opportunity	die Gelegenheit
opposite	das Gegenteil
option subject	das Wahlfach
oral(ly)	mündlich
orange	die Apfelsine
orange juice	der Orangensaft
orchestra	das Orchester

to **order** (i.e. command)	befehlen
to **order** (e.g. a meal)	bestellen
order (i.e. orderliness)	die Ordnung
to **organize**	organisieren
other	ander-
otherwise	sonst
ought	sollen
out of order	außer Betrieb
outskirts	der Stadtrand
over there	drüben
overcast	bedeckt
to **overtake**	überholen
to **own**	besitzen

ABCDEFGHIJKLMNO**P**QRSTUVWXYZ

to **pack**	packen
to **pack** up	einpacken*
packet	das Päckchen; die Packung
page	die Seite
to **paint**	malen
pair	das Paar
pale	blaß
pane	die Scheibe

paper	das Papier
paperback book	das Taschenbuch
parcel	das Paket
pardon?	wie bitte?
parents	die Eltern
park	der Park
to **park**	parken
parking-meter	die Parkuhr
parking-ticket	der Parkschein
part of town	der Stadtteil
participant	der Teilnehmer
partner	der Partner
party	die Party
to **pass** (an exam)	bestehen
to **pass** (hand over)	reichen
passenger	der Passagier
passenger train	der Personenzug
passport	der Paß
passport control	die Paßkontrolle
path	der Pfad; der Weg
patient	der Patient
pause	die Pause
pavement	der Bürgersteig
to **pay**	bezahlen; zahlen
to **pay** attention	achten auf
pea	die Erbse
peach	der Pfirsich
pear	die Birne
pedestrian	der Fußgänger
pedestrian precinct	die Fußgängerzone
to **peel**	schälen
pen-friend	der Brieffreund

pencil	der Bleistift
pensioner	der Rentner
people	die Leute
pepper	das Pfeffer
per	pro
percussion	das Schlagzeug
performance	die Aufführung; die Vorstellung
perhaps	vielleicht
person	der Mensch; die Person
pet	das Haustier
petrol	das Benzin
petrol station	die Tankstelle
photograph	das Foto; die Aufnahme
to **photograph**	fotografieren
physics	die Physik
piano	das Klavier
pickpocket	der Taschendieb
picnic	das Picknick
picture	das Bild
picture postcard	die Ansichtskarte
piece	das Stück
pig	das Schwein
pile	der Haufen
pill	die Pille
pillow	das Kopfkissen
to **pinch** (i.e. steal)	klauen
pink	rosa
pineapple	die Ananas
pipe	die Pfeife

pity!	schade!
place	der Ort; der Platz; die Stelle
place of birth	der Geburtsort
planned	planmäßig
plant	die Pflanze
plaster	das Pflaster
plaster (of Paris)	der Gips
plate	der Teller
platform	der Bahnsteig; das Gleis
play (drama)	das Schauspiel
to **play**	spielen
to **play** skittles	kegeln
to **play** truant	schwänzen
pleasant	angenehm
please	bitte
to **please**	gefallen
plug	der Stecker
plum	die Pflaume
pocket	die Tasche
pocket-money	das Taschengeld
point	der Punkt
police	die Polizei
police station	die Polizeiwache
policeman	der Polizist
polite	höflich
politics	die Politik
poor	arm
pop music	die Popmusik
popular	beliebt
population	die Bevölkerung

pork	das Schweinefleisch
portable	tragbar
porter	der Gepäckträger
portion	die Portion
possible	möglich
to **post**	einwerfen*
post office	die Post; das Postamt
postal code	die Postleitzahl
postal collection	die Leerung
postcard	die Postkarte
poster	das Poster
postman	der Briefträger
pot	das Kännchen; der Topf
potato	die Kartoffel
potato salad	der Kartoffelsalat
pound	das Pfund
to **practise**	üben
to **praise**	loben
precipitation	der Niederschlag
to **prefer**	vorziehen*
to **prepare**	vorbereiten*
present	das Geschenk
to **present**	schenken
pretty	hübsch
previous	vorig
price	der Preis
primary school	die Volksschule
prize	der Preis
probable	wahrscheinlich
problem	das Problem

profession	der Beruf
professional	der Profi
programme	das Programm
programme (TV, radio)	die Sendung
progress	der Fortschritt
to **pronounce**	aussprechen*
proof	der Beweis
prospectus	das Prospekt
protect	schützen
protest	protestieren
Protestant	evangelisch
pub	die Kneipe
public	öffentlich
public holiday	der Feiertag
public house	das Gasthaus; die Wirtschaft; das Wirtshaus
pull	ziehen
pullover	der Pullover (Pulli)
punctual	pünktlich
punishment	die Strafe
purse	das Portemonnaie
to **push**	drücken
to **put**	legen; stecken; stellen
to **put** on (clothes)	anziehen*
pyjamas	der Schlafanzug

quality	die Qualität
quarter	das Viertel
question	die Frage
queue	die Schlange
quick(ly)	schnell
quiet(ly)	leise; still
Quiet!	Ruhe!
quite	ganz; ziemlich

ABCDEFGHIJKLMNOPQ**R**STUVWXYZ

rabbit	das Kaninchen
radio	das Radio
railway	die Eisenbahn
railway crossing	der Bahnübergang
rain	der Regen
to **rain**	regnen
raincoat	der Regenmantel
rainy	regnerisch
rank	der Rang
raspberry	die Himbeere
to **reach**	erreichen
to **read**	lesen
ready	fertig
really	wirklich

receipt	die Quittung
to **receive**	erhalten
recently	neulich
reception	der Empfang
receptionist	die Empfangsdame
recipe	das Rezept
to **reckon**	rechnen
to **recognize**	erkennen
to **recommend**	empfehlen
record	die (Schall-) Platte
record-player	der Plattenspieler
recorder	die Blockflöte
to **recover**	sich erholen
red	rot
red wine	der Rotwein
reduction	die Ermäßigung
refreshments	die Erfrischungen
refrigerator	der Kühlschrank
to **refuel**	tanken
to **refuse**	ablehnen*
region	das Gebiet
regular(ly)	regelmäßig
relative	der/die Verwandte
religion	die Religion
to **remember**	sich erinnern
rent (for house)	die Miete
to **rent**	mieten
repair	die Reparatur
to **repair**	reparieren
to **repeat**	wiederholen
to **repeat** (school year)	sitzenbleiben
report	der Bericht

to **report**	berichten
reservation	die Reservierung
to **reserve**	reservieren
residence	der Wohnort
restaurant	die Gaststätte; das Restaurant
result	das Ergebnis
to **return**	zurückkommen *
return journey	die Rückfahrt
return ticket	die Rückfahrkarte
Rhine	der Rhein
rice	der Reis
rich	reich
to **ride**	reiten
right	recht-
right of way	die Vorfahrt
ring	der Ring
to **ring**	klingeln; läuten; schellen
rissole	die Frikadelle
river	der Fluß; der Strom
to **roast**	braten
roast chicken	das Brathähnchen
roast potato	die Bratkartoffel
roller-skate	der Rollschuh
roof	das Dach
room	der Raum; das Zimmer
room to let	das Fremdenzimmer
round	rund
row (i.e. line)	die Reihe
to **row**	rudern

rowing-boat	das Ruderboot
to **rub**	reiben
to **rub** in	einreiben*
rubber (substance)	der Gummi
rubber (eraser)	der Radiergummi
rucksack	der Rucksack
ruin	die Ruine
ruler	das Lineal
to **run**	laufen; rennen
to **run** over	überfahren
to **rush**	stürzen

ABCDEFGHIJKLMNOPQR**S**TUVWXYZ

sad	traurig
safety-belt	der Sicherheitsgurt
to **sail**	segeln
sailing boat	das Segelboot
sailor	der Matrose
salad	der Salat
salary	das Gehalt
sale	der Ausverkauf
salesperson	der Verkäufer
salt	das Salz
same	gleich

the **same** — dasselbe
sand — der Sand
sandal — die Sandale
sandwich — ein belegtes Brot
satisfactory — befriedigend
satisfied — zufrieden
sauce — die Soße
saucer — die Untertasse
sausage — die Wurst
to **save** (e.g. a person) — retten
to **save** (money) — sparen
to **say** — sagen
to **say** goodbye — sich verabschieden
scarf — der Schal
school — die Schule
school council — die Schülermitverwaltung
school hall — die Aula
school report — das Zeugnis
school yard — der Schulhof
school-bag — die Schultasche
schoolboy — der Schüler
science — die Naturwissenschaft
scooter — der Roller
Scotland/Scotsman — Schottland/Schotte
Scottish — schottisch
scrambled egg — das Rührei
sea — das Meer; die See
seasick — seekrank
season (e.g. football) — die Saison
season (of the year) — die Jahreszeit

second	die Sekunde
secondary modern school	die Hauptschule
secondary school	die Realschule
secretary	die Sekretärin
to **see**	sehen
See you later!	Bis später!
See you soon!	Bis bald!
See you!	Mach's gut!
to **seem**	scheinen
seldom	selten
selection	die Auswahl
self	selbst
self-confident	selbstbewußt
self-service	die Selbstbedienung
self-service (petrol)	Selbsttanken
sell	verkaufen
semi-detached house	das Doppelhaus; das Einfamilienhaus
to **send**	schicken; senden
sender	der Absender
separate(ly)	getrennt
separated	geschieden
to **serve**	dienen
service	die Bedienung
service station	die Raststätte
several	mehrere
to **sew**	nähen
shadow	der Schatten
to **shake**	schütteln
to **share**	teilen
sharp	scharf
to **shave** (oneself)	sich rasieren

shaver	der Rasierapparat
sheep	der Schaf
shelf	das Regal
to **shine**	scheinen
ship	das Schiff
shirt	das Hemd
shoe	der Schuh
shoot	schießen
shop	das Geschäft; der Laden
to **shop**	einkaufen*
shop window	das Schaufenster
shopping basket	der Einkaufskorb
shopping centre	das Einkaufszentrum
shopping trolley	der Einkaufswagen
short	kurz
shoulder	die Schulter
to **shout**	schreien
to **show**	zeigen; vorzeigen*
shower (i.e. in bathroom)	die Dusche
shower (i.e. rain)	der Schauer
to **shower**	sich duschen
shy	schüchtern
sick	krank
side	die Seite
side street	die Nebenstraße
sight (worth seeing)	die Sehenswürdigkeit
sign	das Schild
to **sign**	unterschreiben
signature	die Unterschrift

signpost	der Wegweiser
silk	die Seide
silver	das Silber
similar	ähnlich
simple	einfach
to **sing**	singen
singer	der Sänger
single (unmarried)	ledig
single room	das Einzelzimmer
single ticket	die Einzelkarte
sister	die Schwester
to **sit**	sitzen
to **sit** down	sich (hin-) setzen
situation	die Lage
sixth form	die Oberstufe
skate	der Schlittschuh
to **ski**	Ski fahren (laufen)
skirt	der Rock
sky	der Himmel
skyscraper	das Hochhaus
to **sleep**	schlafen
sleeping bag	der Schlafsack
sleeping car	der Schlafwagen
slice	die Scheibe
slide (film)	das Dia
slim	schlank
slipper	der Pantoffel
sloping	schief
slot	der Einwurf
slow(ly)	langsam
small	klein
smart	schick

to **smell**	riechen
to **smile**	lächeln
to **smoke**	rauchen
smoker	der Raucher
smooth	glatt
snack	der Imbiß
snack-bar	die Imbißstube; der Schnellimbiß
snake	die Schlange
to **sneeze**	niesen
snow	der Schnee
to **snow**	schneien
so	also
soap	die Seife
social studies	die Sozialkunde
sock	die Socke
sofa	das Sofa
sold out	ausverkauft
soldier	der Soldat
some	einige
something	etwas
something or other	irgendetwas
sometimes	manchmal
son	der Sohn
son-in-law	der Schwiegersohn
song	das Lied
soon	bald
sort	die Sorte
soup	die Suppe
sour	sauer
south	der Süden
souvenir	das Andenken

Spain/Spaniard	Spanien/Spanier
Spanish	spanisch
to **speak**	sprechen
special offer	das Sonderangebot
special price	der Sonderpreis
speciality	die Spezialität
spectacles	die Brille
spectator	der Zuschauer
speed	die Geschwindigkeit
to **spell**	buchstabieren
to **spend** (money)	ausgeben *
to **spend** (time)	verbringen
spider	die Spinne
sponge	der Schwamm
spoon	der Löffel
sport	der Sport
sports ground	der Sportplatz
to **spread** (e.g. butter)	streichen
square	der Platz
stadium	das Stadion
staffroom	das Lehrerzimmer
stage	die Bühne
staircase	das Treppenhaus
stairs	die Treppe
stalls (in cinema, etc)	das Parkett
stamp	die Briefmarke
to **stamp**	stempeln
to **stamp** (ticket)	entwerten
to **stand**	stehen
standard lamp	die Stehlampe
star	der Stern
start	der Anfang

to **start**	anfangen*
to **start** (engine)	starten; anlassen*
state	der Staat
station	der Bahnhof
stationer's	die Schreibwaren-handlung
stationery	die Schreibwaren
stay	der Aufenthalt
to **stay**	bleiben
to **stay** overnight	übernachten
to **steal**	stehlen
steamship	der Dampfer
steel	der Stahl
steep	steil
stereo equipment	die Stereoanlage
stew	der Eintopf
stewed fruit	das Kompott
stick	der Stock
to **stick**	kleben
sticking-plaster	das Heftpflaster
still	noch
stocking	der Strumpf
stomach	der Magen
stone	der Stein
stop	die Haltestelle
to **stop**	aufhören*; halten
storey	die Etage; der Stock
storm	der Sturm
stormy	stürmisch
story	die Geschichte
stove	der Ofen
straight	gerade

straight ahead	geradeaus
straw (for drinking)	der Strohhalm
strawberry	die Erdbeere
stream	der Bach
street	die Straße
street map	der Stadtplan
strict	streng
to **strike** (i.e. stop work)	streiken
striped	gestreift
strong	stark
student	der Student
to **study**	studieren
stupid	blöd; dumm; doof
subject (in school)	das Fach
suburb	der Vorort
to **succeed**	gelingen; klappen
success	der Erfolg
suddenly	plötzlich
sufficient	ausreichend
sugar	der Zucker
to **suggest**	vorschlagen*
suit	der Anzug
suitcase	der Koffer
sultry	schwül
summer	der Sommer
summer sales	der Sommerschlußverkauf
summit	der Gipfel
sun	die Sonne
sunbathe	sich sonnen
sunglasses	die Sonnenbrille
sunny	sonnig

sunshine	der Sonnenschein
suntan lotion	das Sonnenöl
supermarket	der Supermarkt
supper	das Abendbrot
sure(ly)	sicher
surgery hours	die Sprechstunde
surname	der Familienname; der Nachname
surprise	die Überraschung
to **surprise**	überraschen
to **swallow**	schlucken
to **sweat**	schwitzen
sweet	süß
sweet	das Bonbon
sweet (final course)	der Nachtisch
sweets	die Süßwaren
swim	schwimmen
swimming baths	das Schwimmbad
swimming cap	die Bademütze
swimming trunks	die Badehose
Swiss	Schweizer/ schweizerisch
switch on	einschalten*
Switzerland	die Schweiz
synthetic material	der Kunststoff

T-shirt	das T-shirt
table	der Tisch
table tennis	das Tischtennis
tablet	die Tablette
to **take**	nehmen
to **take** a seat	Platz nehmen
to **take** care of	aufpassen* auf; pflegen
to **take** off (clothes)	ausziehen*
to **take** off (e.g. weight)	abnehmen*
to **take** part in	teilnehmen* an
to **take** away	wegnehmen*
to **talk**	reden
tap	der Wasserhahn
tape recorder	das Tonbandgerät
target	das Ziel
taste	der Geschmack
to **taste**	schmecken
taxi	das Taxi
tea	der Tee
teacher	der Lehrer
team	die Mannschaft
teapot	die Teekanne
technical high school	die Technische Hochschule
telegram	das Telegramm
telephone	der Fernsprecher; das Telefon
to **telephone**	telefonieren
telephone box	die Telefonzelle
telephone receiver	der Hörer
television	das Fernsehen

television set	der Fernsehapparat; der Fernseher
to **tell**	erzählen
tennis racquet	der Tennisschläger
tense	spannend
tent	das Zelt
term	das Semester
terrace	die Terrasse
terraced house	das Reihenhaus
terrible	furchtbar; schrecklich
test	die Prüfung
to **test**	prüfen
than	als
to **thank**	danken
thank you (very much)	danke (schön)
that's all right	das geht
theatre	das Theater
then	dann
there	da; dort
there and back	hin und zurück
there is; there are	es gibt
thermometer	das Thermometer
thief	der Dieb
thin	dünn
thing	das Ding; die Sache
to **think**	denken; glauben; meinen
thirst	der Durst
to **threaten**	drohen
three-star petrol	Normal
thriller	der Krimi

throat	der Hals
through traffic	der Durchgangs-verkehr
through train	der D-Zug
to **throw**	werfen
thus	also
ticket (for trains, etc)	der Fahrausweis; die Fahrkarte; der Fahrschein
ticket for reserved seat	die Platzkarte
to **tidy** up	aufräumen*
tie	die Krawatte; der Schlips
to **tie**	binden
tiger	der Tiger
tight	eng
tights	die Strumpfhose
time	die Zeit
time (occasion)	das Mal
timetable (transport)	der Fahrplan
timetable (school)	der Stundenplan
tin	die Dose
tin-opener	der Dosenöffner
to **tinker**	basteln
tip	das Trinkgeld
tired	müde
tobacco	der Tabak
today	heute
together	zusammen
toilet	die Toilette; das Klo
tomato	die Tomate
tomorrow	morgen

tongue	die Zunge
tooth	der Zahn
toothbrush	die Zahnbürste
toothpaste	die Zahnpasta
top speed	die Höchstgeschwindigkeit
tortoise	die Schildkröte
to **tow** away	abschleppen*
towel	das Handtuch
tower	der Turm
town	die Stadt
town centre	die Stadtmitte; das Stadtzentrum
town hall	das Rathaus
toy	das Spielzeug
track suit	der Trainingsanzug
trade fair	die Messe
traffic	der Verkehr
traffic jam	die Verkehrsstauung
traffic lights	die Ampel
train	der Zug
to **train**	trainieren
tram	die Straßenbahn
to **transfer**	versetzen
to **translate**	übersetzen
to **travel**	reisen
travel agent's	das Reisebüro
travel information	die Reiseauskunft
to **travel** without paying	schwarzfahren*
traveller	der/die Reisende
traveller's cheque	der Reisescheck
tray	das Tablett

to **treat**	behandeln
tree	der Baum
trophy	der Pokal
trousers	die Hose
trout	die Forelle
trumpet	die Trompete
trunk call	das Ferngespräch
to **try**	versuchen
to **try** (i.e. taste)	probieren
to **try** on	anprobieren*
to **turn** off (the road, etc)	abbiegen*
to **turn off (light, etc)**	ausmachen*; ausschalten*
to **turn** on	anmachen*; einschalten*
TV news	die Tagesschau
twin	der Zwilling
to **type**	tippen
typewriter	die Schreibmaschine
typical	typisch
tyre	der Reifen
tyre pressure	der Reifendruck

ugly	häßlich
umbrella	der Regenschirm
uncle	der Onkel
undecided	unentschieden
underground railway	die U-Bahn
underground station	die U-Bahnstation
to **understand**	verstehen
underwear	die Unterwäsche
unemployed	arbeitslos
unfortunately	leider
unfriendly	unfreundlich
United States	die Vereinigten Staaten
university	die Universität (Uni)
to **unpack**	auspacken*
unpleasant	unangenehm
unusual	ungewöhnlich
upper storey	das Obergeschoß
to **use**	benutzen; gebrauchen
usual (ly)	gewöhnlich
upstairs	oben
urban railway	die S-Bahn
useful	nützlich

vacuum-cleaner	der Staubsauger
valid	gültig
valley	das Tal
VAT	der Mehrwertsteuer
veal	das Kalbfleisch
vegetables	das Gemüse
vehicle	das Fahrzeug
vending machine	der Automat
very	sehr
vet	der Tierarzt
video recorder	das Videogerät
Vienna	Wien
view	die Aussicht
to **view**	besichtigen
village	das Dorf
vinegar	der Essig
violin	die Geige
visit	der Besuch
to **visit**	besuchen
vocational school	die Berufsschule
volleyball	der Volleyball

wage	der Lohn
to **wait**	warten
waiter	der Kellner
Waiter!	Herr Ober!
waiting-hall	der Wartesaal
waiting-room	das Wartezimmer
wake	wecken
wake up	aufwachen*
Wales	Wales
walk	gehen; spazieren
wall (inside)	die Wand
wall (outside)	die Mauer
wallet	die Brieftasche
wallpaper	die Tapete
to **wallpaper**	tapezieren
want	wollen; Lust haben
war	der Krieg
wardrobe	der Kleiderschrank
warm	warm
warning	die Warnung
wash	waschen
wash up	abwaschen*; spülen
washbasin	der Waschbecken
washing	die Wäsche
washing-machine	die Waschmaschine
washing-powder	der Waschpulver
washing-up liquid	das Spülmittel
washroom	der Waschraum
wasp	die Wespe
to **watch** television	fernsehen*
water	das Wasser
water polo	der Wasserball

weak	schwach
weapon	die Waffe
to **wear**	tragen
weather	das Wetter
weather forecast	die Wettervorhersage
weather report	der Wetterbericht
wedding	die Hochzeit
week	die Woche
weekday	der Werktag
weekend	das Wochenende
weekly	wöchentlich
weigh	wiegen
weight	das Gewicht
welcome	Willkommen
Welsh	walisisch
Welshman	Waliser
west	der Westen
West Germany	die BRD
wet	naß
what	was
what a pity!	wie schade!
what sort of ...?	was für ...?
what's missing?	was fehlt?
what's on?	was läuft?
what's up?	was ist los?
wheel	das Rad
when	wann; wenn; als
where	wo
where from	woher
where to	wohin
which	welch-

while	die Weile
whipped cream	die Schlagsahne
white	weiß
white wine	der Weißwein
Whitsun	Pfingsten
who	wer
whole	ganz
why	warum; wozu
wide	breit
widow	die Witwe
wind	der Wind
window	das Fenster
windscreen	die Wind-schutzscheibe
windy	windig
wine	der Wein
wine list	die Weinliste
wish	der Wunsch
to **wish**	wünschen
with breadcrumbs	paniert
witness	der Zeuge
woman	die Frau
wonderful	wunderbar
wood (material)	das Holz
wood	der Wald
wool	die Wolle
word	das Wort
work	die Arbeit
to **work**	arbeiten
worker	der Arbeiter
world	die Welt
world championship	die Weltmeisterschaft

worth seeing	sehenswert
wound	die Wunde
wounded	verwundet
wristwatch	die Armbanduhr
to **write**	schreiben
writing paper	das Schreibpapier
wrong	falsch

ABCDEFGHIJKLMNOPQRSTUVWX**Y**Z

yard	der Hof
year	das Jahr
yellow	gelb
yes	ja
yesterday	gestern
yet	doch
yogurt	der Joghurt
young	jung
young lady	das Fräulein

ABCDEFGHIJKLMNOPQRSTUVWXY**Z**

zoo	der Zoo